To Charlotte

"Merry Christmas"

Best wishes

Jm & Kate
xxx

December 2010.

THE CONTENTED VINE

THE FOOD & WINE BOOK

Kate Preston & Don Morris

Copyright © KATE PRESTON & DON MORRIS

PUBLISHED BY CONTENTED VINE PUBLISHING

ISBN: 978-0-9567560-0-8

"Wines and times at The Contented Vine"

"Twas a woman who led me to drink – I never wrote to thank her"

W.C.Fields

THE CONTENTED VINE

CONTENTS

1. INTRODUCTION — 7
2. STARTERS — 8
3. LIGHT BITES — 12
4. MAINS — 16
5. PUDDINGS — 25
6. KATE'S "ABC OF WINE" — 37
7. DON'S "ART OF THE PARTY" — 44
8. THE GREATEST & OUR FAVOURITE – CHAMPAGNE!! — 51
9. CANAPÉS & PARTY NIBBLES — 56
10. VEGETARIAN DISHES — 60
11. CAKES, BISCUITS, BREADS & PIZZAS — 67
12. DRESSINGS, SAUCES, STOCKS & JAMS — 72
13. OUR MENUS & WINE LISTS — 78
14. CONTENTED CHUMS & SPECIAL THANKS!!! — 81
15. INDEX — 85

THE CONTENTED VINE

CHAMPAGNE ACADEMY PAST CHAIRMEN ANDY HENDERSON, DON HEWITSON, JAMES LYNCH PLUS KEN WILKINS

NICK TARAYAN

OLIVIER DE LA GIRAUDIER & NICOLE SNOZZI

JUSTIN LLEWELYN & JAMES PRICE

ABOVE – DON WITH TWO GREAT CHAMPAGNE MEN: JEAN-MARC CHARLES HEIDSIECK AND CHRISTIAN DE BILLY OF POL ROGER.

RIGHT - KATE WITH DOUG LEEHMANN, PETER LEEHMANN WINES - IN THE BAROSSA VALLEY OZ

1. INTRODUCTION

In March 1996 the late James Lynch took a group of managers from "James Wine bars" to visit Champagne. Amongst them was Kate Preston who was then managing the Orangery Champagne Bar in the City.

Also in Champagne at that time in connection with his promotions and events business, was Don Morris and, through James, they met.

The rest, as they say, is history – a history that resulted in The Contented Vine.

After 12 years we have decided it is time to move on but we wanted to produce a record of The Contented Vine and some of the food and wines that we have served. This book is that and it is for all of you who have been kind enough to ask about our wines and for the recipes – and yes, this includes the recipe for our Baked Chocolate Pudding!!

This book is dedicated to the many friends in the UK food and wine trade and particularly to all our friends, old and new, in Champagne and all the other wonderful wine areas (particularly all our mad wine maker chums in Oz) with whom it has been a pleasure to work, wine and dine!

Our aim was to create a gentle Brasserie that served good freshly prepared food, simple Rotisserie dishes and definitely a great and good value wine list.

The recipes are set out simply, are mostly easy and they work. This is not setting out to be a coffee table glossy but a basically fun book with a few tricks of the trade thrown in that we have tried to keep simple.

From the bombsite that was an old pub called "The Sussex Arms" rose "The Contented Vine" and, in time, The Garden and Red Room downstairs and The Gallery upstairs.

Our thanks again to all our many friends who helped make the CV what it was and we hope you enjoy our food and wine book!

KATE PRESTON & DON MORRIS
PIMLICO, LONDON SW1.
CHRISTMAS 2010

2. STARTERS

CALAMARI

Calamari has been on our menu from day 1. It is a favourite to our customers as an early evening snack with a glass of vino or a starter.

We have always used Squid tubes, which are quite readily available in the freezer section of supermarkets.

The trick for calamari to stop them becoming rubbery is to marinade them in milk for as little as 2 hours. ½ a squid tube is ample for 1 person.
So in this recipe I am not going to give you precise measurements.

Cut your squid tube down each side so you have 2 flat pieces of flesh. Using a sharp knife just score the inside o f the flesh so you have rectangular marks.

Cut the calamari in to the size you wish. Put into a container and cover with milk. Add a crushed clove of garlic.

Let marinate for min 2 hours but no longer than 12. You could now batter the calamari and deep fry. You could dip in seasoned flour and shallow fry. You could char grill – get a griddle preferably or a frying pan really hot. Just lightly brush the griddle with oil and cook for 1 minute each side.

Serve with any of the following a wedge of lemon, aioli, sweet chilli sauce, chickpea puree, etc

CHICKEN LIVER PATE

The simplest of pâtés to make. After I have cut my butter into cubes I put into a dish of iced water and leave in the fridge. The cold butter on the warm livers stops the livers from continuing to cook so is an important part of the process.

1.5 White onion
1 kg chicken livers
325 g cold butter cubed   (1.5 packets)
Chopped fresh garlic
1 shot brandy, port or Madeira.
Step 1
Prepare the chicken livers – cut them in half and take out the central vein.

Step 2
Pan fry the onions till soft with a little garlic and a knob of butter.

Step 3
Add the chicken livers and sauté until brown (2 minutes) – do not overcook!!!

Step 4
Turn off the heat and rest for 5 minutes.

Step 5
Put the livers and the shot of brandy in the blender and add the cold butter cube by cube, until you have a smooth paste.

Put into pate tin and chill overnight.
We line our pate tin with Clingfilm so that it is easy to lift out!

CRAB CAKES

1 lb crab meat
1 egg
1 tbs chopped parsley

1 tbs chopped coriander
1 chilli pepper deseeded and finely chopped
¼ tsp cayenne pepper
½ tsp cumin
Squeeze of lemon
3 oz breadcrumbs (panko Chinese breadcrumbs make a crispier coating)

Step 1
Combine all the ingredients. If a little dry add 1 tbsp mayonnaise.

Step 2
Shape into balls and dip then in breadcrumbs and shallow fry for about 5 mins.
Serve with sweet corn relish.

CROQUETAS JAMON

400g Butter
530g flour
2 litre milk
S & P
Jamon 1oz
1 onion
1 tbsp double cream
breadcrumbs
oil for frying

Step 1
Cut the Jamon into small cubes. You could also use bacon or gammon, but the flavour of dried ham is more intense. Dice the onion. Cook the Jamon and onion together slowly and then allow to cool on paper towels to get rid of the excess fat. Do not let them burn.

Step 2
Make the Béchamel.
Melt the butter and then add the flour till a paste is formed. Slowly add the milk (warm milk can make this bit easier!) little by little. You have to think that you need to give time to the flour to cook - so slowly!!!!!
Add S & P. Add a touch of double cream

Step 3
Add the onion and Jamon mix to the béchamel.

Step 4
Spread the mix onto a flat tray and cover with cling film and allow to cool.

Step 5
Using a spoon shape the béchamel into desired shape or quenelle. Lightly cover with breadcrumbs and deep fry till golden brown. If you can find panko crumbs (Japanese bread crumbs) they will come out even crispier.

Makes enough for 8 portions 32 croquetas.

FRENCH ONION SOUP

Onions are the workhorse of the kitchen. They add such flavour and context to so many dishes. There are also so many different varieties giving different flavours and sweetness. I love French onion soup as it is praise to this fantastic vegetable to have a dish to call its own. Traditionally you would use beef stock for this dish, I prefer to use vegetable stock.

4 large spanish onions
2 red onions
2 white onions (if you can t get these use large shallots)
12 slices mozzarella

6 oz gruyere
2 sprigs rosemary
2 sage leaves
2 bay leaves
4 pints vegetable stock or beef stock
olive oil
2 oz butter
s & p
12 slices of a fat baguette
2 cloves garlic

Step 1
Peel and slice your onions. Cut the onions in half through the root, and slice so that you have semi circular slices.

Step 2
Melt the butter and add 3 tbs olive oil.
Add the onions, 1 garlic bulb and allow the onions to cook. Keep the heat low and gently cook for about 40 minutes until sticky but not burnt. Stir occasionally to prevent sticking to the bottom of the pan.

Step 3
Add the stock and herbs and cook for another 30 minutes.
Your soup is made.
To serve you need to get your cheese toast ready.

Step 4
Lightly Toast the slices of baguette.
Brush them with oil and rub over with garlic. Add some chopped herbs if you wish.

Step 5
Put a slice of mozzarella onto each slice and pop in the oven till melted (5 mins) Grate the Gruyere and put on top of the mozzarella and pop in the oven again until melted. 5 mins

Step 6
In the bottom of each soup bowl put 1 cheese toast. Ladle the soup on the top and then finish off with a cheese toast on the top. Serve.
Serves 6.

TWICE BAKED GOATS CHEESE SOUFFLÉ

200 ml milk
100 gm butter
100 gm flour
6 eggs separated
500 gm goat's cheese
250 gm other cheese (blue or cheddar)

Step 1
Make a roux with the milk, butter and flour.
Melt the butter and add the flour. Stir into a smooth paste with the heat on low. Slowly add the milk a little at a time stirring into a smooth paste each time.

Step 2
Add the egg yolks to the roux then add crumbled cheese and heat until melts. Take off the heat.

Step 3
Beat the egg whites until stiff and add to the cheese mixture.

Step 4
Butter and semolina the Dariole moulds or ramekin dishes.
Put mix in moulds and bake in Bain Marie in mod oven gas 5 for 20 minutes or till golden brown.

These will now keep till required.

Turn out the mould and reheat for 15 mins.
We serve with a little tomato sauce (passata) and olive crostini.

Makes 14

PARMESAN CUSTARD OR PARMESAN BRULÉE

I love making this dish as a starter or instead of a cheese course. You just need to think that you are making savoury custard.

300ml single cream
300ml milk
100g finely grated parmesan cheese
4 egg yolks
cayenne Pepper
S & P

Step 1
Put the cream, milk and parmesan in a bowl and gently heat over a bain marie until all the cheese has melted.

Allow to cool for 20 minutes.

Step 2
Beat the egg yolks till pale in colour add S&P and cayenne and then add to the cheese mixture.

Step 3
Pour into buttered ramekin dishes.

Step 4
The pots of cheese now need to be cooked gently. Put them into an oven proof dish and add boiling water and then put this into an oven for 15 minutes on gas 2/ 150c. a gentle setting.

Step 5
To finish add some more grated cheese and grill for 5 mins or use a blow torch to melt the cheese.
Serve with Anchovy Toast / Rosemary Toast or Melba Toast

3. LIGHT BITES

ARTICHOKE AND GOATS CHEESE TART.

I love making tarts and I add all sorts to the tart mix of eggs and cream depending what is in the larder. This recipe will make 6 small tarts or 1 large 10 in tart.

1 batch of short crust pastry.
8 eggs
500 ml cream
Seasoning
1 tin of artichokes or fresh artichokes peeled and blanched
6 oz goat's cheese
2 tbsp parmesan cheese

Step 1
Roll your pastry and set into a buttered tart tin. Bake blind for 20 mins, gas mark 4. Take the beans off the tart and bake for another 10mins.
Make sure there are no cracks or holes in the pastry. If there are, just plug with a little of the trimmings of the pastry.

Step 2
Chop the artichokes up and place in the pastry case. Roughly break up the goat's cheese. You don't want the hard skin. Add this to the pastry case.

Step 3
Beat the eggs; add the cream and seasoning and beat. Add to the tart case.

Step 4
Sprinkle over some grated hard cheese. I prefer to use Parmesan as it has a strong flavour. Bake in the oven for 30 mins or until golden brown at gas mark 6.

PEA SPINACH AND RICOTTA FILO TART

This recipe will make 6 small tarts or 1 x 10" large tart.

1 Pack filo Pastry 270 ml
4 oz butter
6 eggs
8 oz ricotta
200ml cream
3 0z frozen peas
½ bag baby spinach
2oz hard cheese grated
S & P

Step 1
Melt the butter.
Brush the tart mould with butter and line with 1 sheet of the filo pastry. Then butter and line again with the filo and repeat a 3rd time.

Step 2
Bake the pastry blind for 30 minutes gas 4. (if I am in a hurry and this dish is for a family supper, or I am away and in a kitchen with no baking beans I just bake for 20 mins and let the pastry puff up)

Step 3
Wilt the spinach, and then chop and spread over the pastry case

Step 4
Scatter the peas on the spinach. (You don't need to defrost the peas)

Step 5
Beat the eggs; add the ricotta and seasoning and milk.

Step 6
Add to the pastry case.

Step 7
Sprinkle with the grated cheese and bake for 35 minutes on gas 6.

CHICKEN WINGS

I love chicken wings and they are great as a light snack or as an informal starter.
These really need to marinade for 24 hours – so plan in advance.

12 wings
2 tbs olive oil
3 tbs red wine vinegar (or malt vinegar)
3 tbs soy sauce
s&p

additionally you can add other flavourings like chilli, herbs and tomato paste.

Step 1
Mix the flavourings together into an emulsion. Pour over the wings and swish around – cover and leave in the fridge till you are ready to cook.

Step 2
Heat the oven to gas 5 and put the wings in the oven with the marinade.

Step 3
Cook for 40 minutes – check and turn them over.

Step 4
Pour away the marinade and cook for another 20 minutes. They should go sticky!! Eat!!!

GNOCHI

1 kg potato purée
300g flour
2 eggs
S & P
lemon zest

Step 1
Mix all the ingredients together.

Step 2
Make into a roll and chop.

Step 3
Put into simmering water until they float. Chill down by putting into a bowl of iced water.

Step 4
To serve gently sauté in a little olive oil and serve with your favourite sauce.

POTATO PURÉE

1 kg Potatoes – peeled
300 g Flour
2 eggs
S & P

Step 1
Cook the potatoes and then drain for 20 mins – so they are nice and dry.

Step 2
Add the flour and eggs and make into a dough.

KEDEGEREE

½ onion chopped
55g 2 oz butter
300g 10 ½ oz basmati rice
1 tsp madras powder
¼ tsp nutmeg grated
7 fl oz 200 ml milk
4 fl oz 110 ml cream
300 g smoked haddock
3 boiled eggs
parsley
s & p

Step 1
Poach the haddock in the milk – approx 10 mins.

Step 2
Sauté the onion in the butter.
Add the madras, nutmeg, S&P. Stir.
Add the rice, the milk from the haddock and the cream.
Cover with a lid and on the lowest flame slowly let the rice steam and cook. Turn the flame off after 7 mins. Leave to finish cooking about another 10mins.

Step 3
While the rice is cooking hard boil the eggs for 6 mins.
Peel the eggs and slice into ¼ lengthways.

Step 4
Flake the haddock and add to the rice.

Step 5
Serve, garnishing with the eggs and parsley

PIGEON BREAST A LA PETIT POIS

3 small onions peeled and chopped lengthways in half
2 rashers of streaky bacon, unsmoked
1 clove of garlic
1 tbs cognac
2 pigeon breast
1 bay leaf
½ tin petit pois
1 small glass red wine
tsp butter

Step 1
Fry the onions, garlic and bacon together until the onions are browned.

Step 2
Add the pigeon breast and seal on both sides. (push the onions and bacon to 1 side of the pan.)

Step 3
Add the cognac – deglaze

Step 4
Add the peas, red wine and bay leaf and cook for about 3 minutes – pigeon breast should still be slightly pink and the peas hot.

Step 5
Add the knob of butter to finish and give gloss.

Serves 2 as a starter or 1 for a main course.

PORK PIE

This is my friend Daphne's recipe and I remember her making this when I was a child. It's great to make at Christmas if you are having a large amount of guests round.

8 oz belly pork
8 oz pork loin
¼ tsp nutmeg
1 tbsp sage

1 tbsp thyme
1 tbsp parsley
1 tbsp worcester sauce
1 tbsp soy
1 tsp tomato paste
S & P

Hot Water Crust Pastry
1lb strong white flour
6oz lard
¼ pt water
½ tsp salt

Jelly
2 pigs trotters
bouquet garni
3 pints water

Step 1
Make the jelly
Cleave the pigs trotters down the centre, put in a big pot with bouquet garni and water on the heat and simmer for 2 ½ hours.

Step 2
Mince your pork – or you can chop finely. You need some fat in the mix.
To taste add your herbs and spices. I have given the amounts that I generally use, but please add more or less.

Step 3
Make the pastry
Sieve the flour into a bowl.
Boil the lard in the water and pour into the flour.
Mix and knead well.
Allow to cool a little for about 10 mins but don't put in the fridge.

Step 4
Cut approx a ¼ of the pastry and keep aside for the lid.

Step 5
Grease a 5 in high sided pastry tin.
Roll out the pastry. It is quite strange to handle as it is still warm. You will need plenty of flour on your pin and rolling surface.

Step 6
Line your tin with the pastry. Push the pastry into the edges and over the top.

Step 7
Put your meat in the pastry case.

Step 8
Roll out the pastry for the lid. Cut a small circle in the middle. Put on top of the pie and crimp the edges together.
If you are feeling artistic you could cut some leaves etc out of the trimmings.

Step 9
Bake in the oven gas mark 5 for 1 ½ hours.

Step 10
Check to see if cooked.
Turn out of the tin and cook on a baking tray for another 30 mins.

Step 11
Finish making your jelly.
Sieve the stock

If you don't like the thought of pigs trotters you can always cheat by making a veg stock and add 3 gelatine leaves.

If you don't like the jelly you could just leave this step out completely.

Step 12
Take the pie out of the oven and allow to cool for 1 hour.

Step 13

Pour the jelly into the hole at the top of the pie. If the jelly has started to set, just re heat so that it becomes liquid again.
Allow to chill overnight and serve.

4. MAINS

BURGERS

I love a good burger and love to make them with all the trimmings. You have to have good meat to create a good burger. I go along to my butcher and, in a perfect world, I will choose a piece of sirloin with the lovely creamy fat and either some rump (if I am feeling rich!) or some chuck steak. I will then ask my butcher to mince this through his machine. I like my burgers fairly coarse so will just put the meat through once, but if you like a finer mince ask him to put through twice.

I work on 8oz per person then season my meat with salt and pepper and I will also chop ½ an onion really finely and add this to the mix. Form into rounds.

The burgers are ready to grill!!!

I also make **MINI BURGERS** as a canapé from this mix. Each mini burger is approx 1oz.
We use a pastry cutter to get a good round shape and grill in the same way. To serve the mini burgers we use English muffins, toasted and then using the same cutter cut the rounds out of the muffins. I like using muffins as they have a good crust!

I like to serve ours with a spread of guacamole on the muffin, the burger and then garnish with tomato relish/ sweet corn relish and a Wally/ gherkin.

Guacamole
1 avocado
1tsp lemon juice
dash of Tabasco

Put all the ingredients into a bowl and mix.

This is very simple – for the mini burger I want a smooth paste. If this was to be used as a dip I would add in 3 chopped spring onions, and 1 tomato chopped fine.

COQ AU VIN

This is one of my all time favourite dishes. The recipe I use I have developed for speed of preparation but also as it works with young spring chicken. I would not know where to go to get a Coq!!!

In my view the wine used for this dish doesn't need to be fantastic, but it does need to be gusty. Look for a French country wine or a cabernet sauvignon.

1 large chicken cut into 8 pieces.
(when I do this for a buffet dish I use Skin on Breast with the wing bone still in 6 breast pieces cut in half)
1 bottle of wine
1 Spanish onion diced
2 cloves garlic
12 shallots peeled
8 oz streaky bacon chopped into small pieces
Rosemary, bay, sage and thyme bouquet garni
2 tbsp vegetable oil
6 oz mushrooms
2 oz Chicken liver chopped small

Step 1
Marinade the chicken with the onion the garlic and the bottle of wine for 24 hours.

Step 2
Get your frying pan hot.
Add half the oil and start browning your chicken. Skin side down first and then turn. Make sure you have a lovely golden brown.

Put the chicken into a heavy pot.

Step 3
Deglaze the pan with some of the wine marinade and add to the pot.

Step 4
Get your pan really hot again and gently fry off the bacon and cook till crisp and brown. Add to the pot.

Step 5
In the bacon fat fry off the shallots whole – until a good colour.
Add to the pot.

Step 7
Deglaze the pan with some of the wine marinade.

Step 8
Quickly fry the chicken livers and add to the pot. Deglaze.

Step 9
Add the bouquet garni and any of the marinade that is left and bring the pot to bubbling.

Step 10
I then turn off the coq au vin and like to leave to marinade a good 6 hours more.

Step 11
Put the chicken on the hob or in the oven and cook for 30 minutes or until the chicken is tender.

Step 12
Add the mushrooms and cook for a further 10 minutes.

If you like the sauce thicker, take out the meat and the onion and reduce the sauce down, or thicken using a little corn flour. (I quite like my sauce thin so never bother with this stage. I like the sauce to absorb into the rice or mash or even a thick slice of bread!!)

The definitive guide to coq au vin is the Elizabeth David recipe.

FISHCAKES

This dish has been on our menu since we opened.

I have given you quantities for a serving of 6 – 18 fishcakes in total. You can of course play with the herbs etc you use and use less or more.

You obviously can just make the 1 flavour of fishcake, especially if you have some fish left over from something else.

You need to think in proportions – you need twice the amount of potato to fish as a rule of thumb.
Our combinations were
Salmon with Dill,
Cod with Parsley
Smoked Haddock.

Step 1
Boil the potatoes in salted water till cooked and leave to drain.

Step 2
At the same time roast the fish in a moderate oven gas 5. Cover in foil while roasting.

Step 3
Mash your potatoes - do not add any butter or milk. The idea is to get a dry mash. Check the seasoning at his point and add some more salt if necessary. Split equally into 3 bowls.

Step 4
Flake the 3 different fishes - checking for bones and add each of the fishes to the 3 bowls of mash.

Step 5
Chop your herbs small and add to each of the bowls.
Dill with the salmon.
Parsley with the cod.

Step 6
Mix each bowl until all the ingredients are thoroughly combined.

Step 7
Form your cakes.
We use a round mould 4 cm in diameter.
Take a handful of the mixture and press into the ring until tightly packed.
Continue until all the mixture is finished.

At this point you could store the cakes until you are ready to cook. They will hold happily for 12 hours. Store them in a Tupperware box using greaseproof paper in between the layers.

Step 8
Heat your frying pan. Dip the fishcakes in seasoned flour.
Add the oil and fry on both sides for 3 minutes.
Keep warm in a moderate oven till you have fried the whole batch. Serve with the Spinach cream sauce and a crisp salad.

You could also dip the fishcakes into egg and breadcrumb and cook in the same way.
Try panko crumbs – Japanese breadcrumbs.

SPINACH FISHCAKE SAUCE

1 ½ oz 40g flour
1 ½ oz 40g butter
½ pint milk
4 tbs white wine
4 tbs fish stock
4 oz spinach

Step 1
Make a béchamel. Melt the butter and add the flour and stir into a paste. Slowly add the milk, continuing to stir. Add the wine and stock.
And cook for a further 5 minutes.

Step 2
Cut the spinach into thin strips.

Step 3
Just before serving add the spinach.

FRESH PASTA

Fresh pasta is very easy to make - but I do reserve it for special occasions or when I have some children around to help put it through the pasta maker.

The pasta dough needs to be made a few hours in advance.

1¼ cups flour
2 eggs
½ tsp olive oil
polenta for dusting

Step 1
Put 1 cup of flour into a bowl and make a well in the centre. Add the eggs, and olive oil into the well and using a fork, lightly beat the eggs incorporating the flour as you go.

Step 2
Turn the dough onto a floured surface adding the remaining flour as needed. The dough needs to be kneaded for about 8 mins until it is smooth and glossy. Split into 4 and wrap in cling and set aside for at least 30 mins.

And now for the fun part.

Step 3
Set the pasta rollers at its widest setting. Flatten the dough slightly and feed through the machine. Fold into 1/3rd s and repeat twice. Move to the next setting and pass the dough thru. Repeat until you are on the smallest setting.

My favourite is linguini – but now pass the flat dough through the cutter you desire. Dust lightly with polenta or cornmeal to prevent sticking.

When you have finished – cook the pasta it will only take 20 seconds – and serve with your favourite sauce.

You can keep this wrapped in the fridge for a week. Or even dry it and keep in an airtight jar.

serves 4 as a main course

IBIZAN LAMB

This is a great traditional dish from the Ibiza countryside that we sometimes served in the Garden. A glorious dish for Sunday lunch!

1 shoulder of lamb
2 green peppers
I red onion
2 tomatoes
3 pints veg stock
s & p
olive oil
waxy potatoes about 5

Step 1
Get the frying pan really hot. Add the olive oil and then fry the lamb shoulder turning until browned.

Step 2
Put in a casserole dish and cover with the veg stock, place in oven and cook slowly. After 1 hour skim the casserole dish.

Step 3
Add the sliced pepper and tomatoes quartered.
Add peeled waxy potatoes.
Cover the pot again and cook slowly for another hour and half.

At this point the lamb should be really tender. You may want to take the meat and veg out and slightly thicken the sauce. However this is not necessary.

INDIVIDUAL PARMEGIANI MELANZONE

This is great for vegetarians.

6 beef tomatoes
1 spanish onion
1 aubergine
1 tbs tomato paste
1 egg
1 tbs flour
olive oil
1 mozzarella round
6 basil leaves

Step 1
Cut the top of the tomatoes and scoop out the flesh.

Step 2
Sauté the onions and add the insides of the tomatoes and tomato paste, s& p and cook for 5 minutes. Whilst this is cooking...

Step 3
Slice the aubergine into 3mm slices. Dip into the flour and then into the beaten egg and shallow fry on both sides.

Step 4
Assemble the tomato. Fill the tomato in layers Aubergine, Tomato sauce, basil leaf, mozzarella.

You can keep in the fridge at this point until you are ready to serve.

Bake for 15 minutes gas mark 7.

LAMB TAGINE

2lb lamb cut into cubes.
1 tbs ground cardamom
1 tbs ground cumin
1 tsp ginger
6 tbs olive oil
1 parsnip peeled and cubed
2 carrots peeled and diced
1 onions peeled and diced
¼ cup tomato paste
1 cup red wine
¼ cup Madeira or sherry
1 cups meat stock
1 cup dates/ prunes/ apricots (optional)
1 tbs lemon juice or preserved lemon
bouquet garni- rosemary, thyme, bay leaf.
S & P

Step 1
Season the meat with the S&P and half of the cumin and cardamom. Rub the meat with the spices and then leave for 2 hours so the meat can absorb the flavours.

Step 2
Heat the saucepan; add the oil and brown the meat – do this in batches if necessary.
Put the browned meat into the Tagine or casserole dish.

Step 3
Sweat the onions, parsnip and carrots.

Step 4
Add the remaining spices and the tomato paste. Add the wine and sherry and bring to the boil and reduce by half.

Step 5
Add this to the Tagine / casserole dish. Add the stock, lemon juice, fruit and bouquet garni, and simmer in the oven for 2 hours.

Serve with cous cous.

I also make a **MUSHROOM TAGINE.** Just replace the meat with mushrooms. – I like a range of different ones and I especially like chestnut mushrooms.

Use the same method, but you will only need to cook the tagine for 45 mins.

NORMANDY PORK

My dad started to learn to cook when I was in my teens, and he mastered a few dishes that became family favourites. This is one of them and my staff like me to cook this sometimes for their staff lunch. It,s very quick and easy!!

Serves 6
2 onions
2 pork fillet or loin approx 2lb
6 cooking apples
4 oz butter
1 pint cider
¼ pint cream

Step 1
Slice your onions. Cut the onion in half and slice so you have long thin pieces of onion. Peel your apples and slice - ¼ them and core the apples and slice lengthways.

Step 2
Sauté the onions in the butter till soft and they begin to colour.

Step 3
Add the apples and stir and let cook with the onions for about 2 minutes.

Step 4
Add the cider and bring to the boil.

Step 5
Sauté off the meat in a separate frying pan to give a little colour.

Step 6
10 mins before serving add the pork to the cider and apple mix and allow to simmer for 5 - 10 mins. If you are using loin trim the fat off.

Step 7
Add the cream just before serving.
We used to have loads of mash with this dish to mop up the rich cider and apple sauce.

I make mine without the cream at the end!!

PORK BELLY

This dish needs to be prepared 2 days in advance.
1 whole pork belly
3 tbs rock salt
3 sprigs rosemary
1 spanish onion
2 cloves of garlic

Step 1
Score the skin of the pork belly.
Rub the salt and rosemary on both sides of the pork belly. (If you wish for a Chinese style – rub in some 5 spice)
Leave in the fridge for 24 hours to marinade.

Step 2
Put your roasting tray in the oven and get really hot. Add your sliced onion and garlic with some vegetable oil. Put in the oven for 10 mins.
Add the pork onto the onions skin down.
Roast for 4 hours in a slow oven, gas 3.

Step 3
Allow to cool. Take the pork out of the tray and just pull the bones out whilst still warm.
Discard the onions. Put the pork back in the tray with the skin up. Cover in foil and you need to weigh the meat down (we use a dozen plates) to get rid of the excess fat.

Leave for at least 6 hours.

Step 4
Cut into squares.

Step 5
When you are ready to serve – put a tray in the oven to get really hot. Place the pork on the tray – skin down and cook in the oven for 10 mins.
Turn the pork over and cook for another 15mins.
Serve with your favourite veg.

Serves 12

RAGU

1 Large onion diced
2 celery sticks diced
1 carrot diced
350 g mince meat
250 ml white wine
8 tbsp milk
½ tsp nutmeg
400g tinned tomatoes
3 tbsp olive oil
40g butter

Step 1
Sauté the onions in the oil and butter till translucent. Add the celery and carrots and sauté for another 2 mins.

Step 2
Add the mince meat and cook till the meat has just lost its rawness.

Step 3
Add the wine and cook until the wine has evaporated a little – about 5 mins.

Step 4
Turn the heat down to medium and add the milk. Cook until the milk has evaporated.

This is a critical step – the lactic acid in milk helps to soften the beef.

Step 5
Add the tomatoes and nutmeg. When this starts to bubble turn the heat down as low as possible and cook for 3 hours. Stirring occasionally.

If I want a less tomatoey sauce I will add beef stock and just add a tbsp of tomato puree, instead of the tinned tomatoes.

Serves 6

ROAST CHICKEN WITH SWEETCORN AND GINGER STUFFING

Stuffing
I tin sweet corn
2 celery stalks
1 onion
2 cm piece of fresh ginger
1 cup breadcrumbs
1 egg
1 oz butter

Chicken
1 Corn fed chicken
6 shallots
Juice of 1 lemon
2 oz butter

Step 1
In a bowl with the breadcrumbs add the onion mix, sweet corn and egg and mix together.

Step 2
Stuff the bird with this mix.

Step 3
Pour the lemon juice over the chicken and put the lemon in the cavity. Smear the butter all over the chicken and put in a roasting dish.

Step 4
Cut the ends of the shallots off and put in the roasting dish around the chicken. Roast for 15 mins at gas 8 and then turn down to gas 4 and continue to roast for another hour.

Serve with roast potatoes!!

STEAK PIE

This is a very simple dish to prepare but takes a little time to cook. Great in the winter and serve with roasted winter vegetables and mash.

If you like kidneys with your pie add about 3 oz to this recipe and cook them with the meat covered in flour. This makes a pie for 4

1.5 lb chuck steak
1 large onion
2 mushrooms
pastry – short crust or puff
flour
S & P

Step 1
Cut the meat into cubes and cut the onion into slices.

Step 2
Toss the meat and the onion with the seasoned flour, so that it is evenly coated.
Put this in a casserole dish.

Step 3
Cover the meat with vegetable stock and ½ a cup of red wine. Seal the dish and put in a moderate oven for 1.5 hours.

Step 4
Taste the meat – it should be nice and tender, if not cook for a further 20 mins.

Step 5
Put the meat into a dish, add the sliced mushroom and cover with a pastry lid. Cook for another 40 mins or until the pastry is cooked – gas 8.

Serves 6

THE FAMILY CHICKEN PIE

We love this in the Wilcox (mums maiden name) family – a great way to use up the remains of a roast chicken or turkey.
Pickings of the roast chicken or poach some chicken until cooked.

Stuffing mix
Béchamel Sauce
Puff Pastry

Put the chicken into a pie dish. Rehydrate the stuffing mix and make into balls. Fry these until nicely browned. Put in the pie dish with the chicken. If you wish you can add mushrooms, crispy bacon (I also like sweet onion marmalade)

Add the béchamel sauce.

Roll out the puff pastry and cover the pie dish (Tip. Make sure the pastry goes over the dish. I then add the trimmings of the pastry around the edge in a strip. This stops the pastry sagging into the pie)

Brush with an egg yolk. Cook for about 30 minutes.

BÉCHAMEL SAUCE

1 tablespoon butter
1 heaped tablespoon flour
½ pint milk.
Salt and pepper.

Melt the butter and add the flour. Keeping the pan on the stove mix and stir with a wooden spoon until you have a smooth paste.

Béchamel sauce needs to be cooked slowly to allow time for the flour to cook. Don't rush.

Slowly add the milk a splash at a time. Each time coming back to the smooth consistency. Otherwise you will end up with a lumpy sauce!!!

Add s & p to taste.

Don is not a huge fan of béchamel sauce so I make another version replacing the béchamel with chicken gravy.

CHICKEN GRAVY.

Boil up the carcass of chicken with an onion – Just chop an onion in half leaving the skin on. Use enough water to cover the bones

After about an hour and a half remove the bones and strain through a sieve. Add a thickener – gravy granules or corn flour.

5. PUDDINGS

AMERICAN CHEESECAKE

Mum bought this American recipe back from Canada and it has been a family favourite ever since.

Biscuit base
8 oz digestive biscuits (or ginger if you fancy)
3 oz melted butter

Cheese mix
1 lb cream cheese
2 eggs
3 oz castor sugar
1 ½ tsp vanilla essence or ½ tsp vanilla extract

Sour cream topping
½ pint sour cream
1 level tbsp caster sugar
1 tsp vanilla essence or ¼ tsp vanilla extract

Step 1
Make the biscuit base.
Crush the biscuits and add the melted butter. Line an 8 in cake tin and press the biscuit mix into the bottom. Put in the fridge while you make the cheesecake.

Step 2
Beat the cheese to soften, add the eggs and beat till smooth.
Add the sugar and vanilla.
Pour the mixture onto the biscuit base.

Bake in the oven for 25 mins at gas 5. Take the cheesecake out and increase the heat to gas 8.

Step 3
Mix the sour cream, caster sugar and vanilla together.

Carefully pour this mixture over the cheesecake and return to the oven for 5 mins. The cake can burn if in the oven for any longer!!!! Chill and serve!!

Serves 12

BAKED CHOCOLATE PUDDING

This has to be everyone's favourite – otherwise known as Chocolate Fondant.

250g dark chocolate
250 g butter
4 eggs
4 egg yolks
6 heaped tablespoons of plain flour
46g castor sugar

Step 1
Melt the butter and chocolate over a Bain Marie.

Step 2
While you wait for the chocolate to melt – you need to get your pudding moulds prepared. Butter the mould with melted butter, and then flour it. Butter the mould again and flour again. This is extremely important. If the mould is not buttered and floured twice, the fondant will stick and not come out of the mould.

Step 3
Get your eggs ready. The yolks add to the sugar and mix. The whites (only 4) whisk till frothy (not stiff).

Step 4
Add the sugar and egg yolks to the chocolate, then the flour and then the egg whites. You should have a lovely chocolate mixture.

Step 5
Pour the mix into the prepared moulds.
Chill in the fridge until needed.

Cook for 12 minutes in moderate oven. Ready when a crust has formed over the top. Turn out onto a serving plate and serve with ice cream, cream, coulis etc

You will need Dariole moulds or Ramekin dishes (not as good as they are not as deep)

The secret for this working is the double butter and flouring of the mould. To do this have some melted butter and using a pastry brush wipe the melted butter around the mould. Put about a ½ teaspoon of flour into the mould and turn the mould so that the flour sticks to the butter. Repeat. If you don't do this twice the pudding will not drop out easily.

You also might want to experiment first to get the cooking time right. Everyone's ovens are slightly different. But it is cooked when the surface has crusted over – too long and it will set in the middle and not ooze.

I love this with ice cream!!!!
This recipe will make about 12.

BREAD AND BUTTER PUDDING

8 stale croissant / bread/ pannetone
4oz sultanas
8 egg yolks
200 g sugar
2 pints milk

Serves 10

Step 1
Make the custard
Put the milk on to boil, meanwhile whisk your egg yolks with the sugar.
When milk has just reached boiling take off the heat and let stand for 5 mins, add to the sugar and eggs and return to the pan and gently whisk. You will feel a thickening, at that stage pull off the heat.
WARNING: DO not let the mixture boil or it will turn into scrambled eggs.

Step 2
Butter your bread and then dip into the custard mixture and start layering into a tray about 2 in deep.

Add sultanas (or any other dried fruit) as you layer.

Step 3
Pour the remaining custard over the dish and bake in a moderate oven for 30mins.
Serves 8

CHERRY AND ALMOND TART

I love making this tart as you look clever but don't have to make any pastry!!!

500g butter
500g sugar
50g ground almonds
10 eggs
500g sieved flour
fresh cherries halved and stoned (or any other fruit of the season - plums, pears, apples work well)

Step 1
Beat the butter and sugar till creamed. They should be light and fluffy.

Step 2
Fold in the Almonds, then the eggs and then the flour.

Step 3
Butter and line the tart dish you wish to use.

Step 4
Pour in the mixture. And decorate with the cherries cut side up.

Step 5
Bake in the oven in a cool oven 150 gas mark ¾ for 12 minutes.

Red Wine Syrup
This goes really well as a garnish.
500ml red wine
250g sugar

Simmer till reduced by half.

CHOCOLATE POT

This dessert has been on our menu for as long as I can remember and is a great little dessert to finish off a meal or to have with red wine!!!

200 gm melted dark chocolate (70% cocoa solids)
70 gm melted butter
zest of 1 orange
6 eggs
80gms sugar

Step 1
Melt your chocolate with the butter in a bowl over a pan of hot water.

Step 2
Separate your eggs.
Whisk the egg yolks with the sugar.

Step 3
Whisk your egg whites till almost stiff.

Step 4
Add the egg yolks to the chocolate and mix together. Add the whites and orange zest and stir in.

Put into little pots and chill to set.

CHOCOLATE SAUCE FOR ICE CREAM

50g cocoa powder
50g castor sugar
100ml water

75ml cream

Step 1
Whisk the cocoa, sugar and water into a smooth paste.

Step2
Bring to the boil and cook gently for 3 minutes stirring consistently.

Step 3
Take off the heat, add the cream, serve !!

CHOCOLATE TART

Sweet Pastry
265 gm 9 oz butter
120 gm 5 oz icing sugar
3 egg yolks
340 gm 12 oz flour

12" dish

Step 1
Make the pastry.
Put all ingredients into food processor until combined. Wrap in cling film and chill.

Step 2
Grease a 12" pastry case. Roll out the pastry and put in the pastry tin. Line with greaseproof paper and add your cooking beans and bake the pastry blind for 20 mins gas mark 4. Take off the beans and bake for a further 10 mins.

Filling
6 egg yolks
4 whole eggs
80 gm 3oz castor sugar
300gm 10 oz butter
400 gm 14 oz chocolate

Step 1
Melt butter and chocolate in Bain Marie.

Step 2
Beat sugar and eggs vigorously until frothy.

Step 3
Mix the chocolate mixture with the egg mix until amalgamated.

Step 4
Pour into pastry case and put in oven for 10 minutes gas 3 250c

Allow to cool.

LEMON TART

1 x 12" Sweet pastry case
600 ml double cream
5 egg yolks
juice of 8 lemons
92 Gms sugar

Step 1
Dissolve the sugar with the lemon juice.

Step 2
Put the cream and eggs into a bowl and place on a Bain Marie.

Step 3
Add the sugar and lemon solution and whisk for 5 mins.

Step 4
Pour into pastry case and cook for 10 minutes in a cool oven gas 4.

Allow to cool.

MARQUISE CHOCOLATE CAKE

240 g Butter
360g Dark Chocolate melted
290g Moscavado sugar
5 Eggs
Caramel brittle

Step 1
Melt the chocolate and butter over a Bain Marie.

Step 2
Melt the sugar in 4 tbsp hot water.

Step 3
Beat the egg whites till stiff.

Step 4
Add the sugar to the chocolate. Mix. Add the egg yolks. mix. Add the egg whites in 3 stages, mixing each time.

Step 5
Line and grease an 8" cake tin.

Step 6
Pour 2/3rds of the mixture into the tin and bake for 30 minutes.

Step 7
Allow to cool for about 30 mins and add the caramel brittle. Pour the last of the chocolate into the cake tin and bake for another 20 mins.

CARAMEL BRITTLE

8 oz sugar
1 tsp water
2 oz Crushed almonds or nuts of your choice

Step 1
Put the sugar and water in a sauce pan and heat till brown.

Step 2
Add the crushed nuts.

Step 3
Line a tray with clingfilm and spread the mixture on this and chill.

Step 4
Crack in to desired size pieces.
I like mine quite small.

PAVLOVA

Delicious in the summer and a great way to use up egg whites.

12 egg whites
24oz castor sugar
4 tsp vinegar
3 tbs corn flour

No corn flour for meringue.

Step 1
Beat your eggs till stiff

Step 2
Add the sugar a tablespoon at a time and continue beating.

Step 3
Add the vinegar and corn flour.

Step 4
Spread the mix onto a greased greaseproof lined baking tray in any shape you wish. I like to use a piping bag and make them into individual rounds. The sides should be higher than the middle so that you can fill easily.

Step 5
Bake in a cool oven for about 30 mins to an hour or until they are just turning in colour. Ideally turn the oven off and leave them in the oven with the door slightly open.

Step 6
Fill with cream and any fruit or nuts of your choice.

Note.
To make meringue leave the Corn flour out and they will be crisp throughout. Makes 4" to 8" in pavlova.

ITALIAN DACQUIRE

This is an Italian wedding cake but great for buffets.

Step 1
Make your Pavlova as above.

I used a plate to draw a circle on the greaseproof paper as a template and then greased the paper. I also use a piping bag – I find it easier.

You will need 4 Pavlova's. The recipe above will make this many. The Pavlova's can be made 2 days before and stored in a dry place.

Crème Pâtissière
10 egg yolks
150 g caster sugar
50 g corn flour
600 ml milk

Step 1
Bring your milk to the boil.

Step 2
Beat the yolks, sugar and corn flour in a bowl.

Step 3
Add the milk to the egg mix and whisk.

Step 4
Pour the mixture back into the saucepan and continue to heat – stirring all the time.
It will suddenly thicken. At this point take it off the heat and continue to whisk and voila crème Pâtissière!

Allow to cool for 10 minutes and put into your piping bag.

TIP: Use a jug to support your piping bag – easier to fill.

Step 5
1 pint cream
3 tbs sieved icing sugar
Whisk your cream and sugar till stiff.

Step 6
1 x punnet strawberries
2 x punnets raspberries

Hull your strawberries and cut in half (you can use more or less depending on how much fruit you want). Assemble.

Put one Pavlova on a serving plate.

Pipe on half of the crème Pâtissière and place the raspberries around the edge.

Place a Pavlova on the top of this.

Mix half the cream with the strawberries (leaving some strawberries for decoration) put the cream on top of the Pavlova (leaving a large spoonful for the top.)

Another Pavlova

Another layer of Crème Pâtissière and raspberries. Add the final Pavlova and decorate with the remaining fruit and crème.

PROFITEROLES

2½ ozs / 60gms flour
1 tsp sugsr
2 oz / 50gms butter
2 eggs beaten

makes about 14

Step 1
Get all your ingredients measured out.
Sieve the flour onto some greaseproof paper with the sugar, so that it is to hand.
Have you eggs beaten and ready.

Step 2
Greaseproof and butter a tray. Put the greaseproof paper under the tap to moisten and then shake off any excess water. Put this back onto your tray.

Step 3
Get your piping bag ready – quick tip use a jug and put your piping bag into this and fold the piping bag over the jug, so that you can easily pour the paste into the bag.

Step 4
Melt the butter with the water.

Step 5
Add the flour and sugar and beat until smooth.
Take off the heat!!!

Step 6
Add your eggs a bit at a time and incorporate into the mixture.

Step 7
Put the sloppy dough into the piping bag.

Step 8
Pipe balls onto the greased paper, until all the paste is finished.

Step 9
Get a cup of water and dip your finger into the water and just press onto the piped ball – you will get rid of all the peaks of the dough this way and also add a little water which will help with the forming of the profiterole.

Step 10
Put in a moderate oven at mark 6 and cook for 20 minutes (check them after 15 mins)
They should puff up and be a lovely caramel colour.

Step 11
Take out of the oven and most importantly skewer every profiterole in the side – this takes the air out and stops them from going soggy. Also gives you a hole to fill them with.

Allow to cool.

You can keep them for 3 day in an airtight container.

Fill them using a piping bag and nozzle with

Crème Pate
Chocolate Grenache
Caramel Sauce
Chantilly Cream

Stack them on a plate and drizzle some filling over the top and dust with icing sugar.

To make a croquembouche you need a wizard's hat and many more profiteroles. I garnish with spun sugar.

STEAM PUDDING

This was the first dish I learnt to cook as a very young girl and we would have this most Sundays for pudding. You can use any jam you like or golden syrup, or honey etc

4oz butter
4 oz self raising flour, Sieved
1 tsp baking powder
4 oz caster sugar
2 eggs
3 Tbsp Jam / syrup

Step 1
Grease a 1 ½ Pint Pudding Bowl.

Step 2
Put your jam in the bottom of the basin.

Step 3
Cream your butter and sugar, add the eggs and beat and then add the flour and baking powder and beat. Put the mixture into the pudding basin, on top of your jam.

Step 4
Take a large piece of foil and put a pleat in to it. Secure the foil tightly around the basin with the pleat in the middle of the pudding to allow for expansion.

Step 5
Place the pudding in a large saucepan with water coming half way up the basin. Simmer for 1½ hours.

Step 6
Turn out onto a plate and serve with custard or cream.

Serves 6/8. You can also make a **suet pudding** which is slightly heavier.

1 cup milk
1 tsp lemon juice
1 cup suet
1 tsp baking powder
2 cups flour

Step 1
Grease your pudding basin.

Step 2
Add the lemon juice to the milk.
Add all the other ingredients and mix together.

Step 3
Put any jam etc in the bottom of the basin and add the mixture. Steam as before.

TARTE TATIN

I love making these, they require very little equipment and I have often made them, to my guests delight, on holiday with a very basic kitchen.

There are 2 ways on the stove or in the oven.
I am not going to give you precise quantities.
You basically require apples or pears 1.5 per person.

Butter about 3 oz per person
Sugar about 1 tbs per person
Puff pastry.

On the stove you need to use a frying pan, in the oven you need to use a circular baking dish, tart dish (or if you want to make individual ones I used those brown Spanish clay dishes.)

Step 1
Blanket the bottom of your cooking vessel with sugar.

Step 2
Slice your butter into approx 3mm slices. And place a layer onto the sugar.

Step 3
Peel your fruit and cut into 1/8ths.

Step 4
Arrange the wedges on top of the butter. I start from the outside and work in. You want to try and fit as much fruit in as possible – it really does shrink.

Step 5
On the Stove: put the frying pan under the heat. when top starts to bubble lower the heat and keep cooking for about another 40 minutes.

They are ready when the apples have turned golden and sticky. It is very easy to catch at the end so keep and eye on it for the last 10 mins.

In the oven:
Put in an oven. This will take slightly longer than on the stove about 1.5 hrs. Again don't let them catch. Allow to cool.

Step 6
Cut the puff pastry to fit your dish.
Place on the apples and tuck the pastry inside the dish.

Step 7
Bake in moderate oven till the pastry is brown.

Step 8
Put a plate on the top of the Tart and turn over.

Serves 6

ICE CREAM

8 egg yolks
1 pint milk
1 pint dbl cream
200 gm sugar
I vanilla pod

Makes 1 litres

Step 1
Slice the vanilla pod down the centre and using a knife scrape the seeds into the milk and cream. Add the pod.
Bring the cream and milk to the boil.

Step 2
In the meantime whisk the sugar and eggs together.

Step 3
Add the heated milk to the eggs and whisk.

Put the egg and milk mixture back on the stove and gently, stirring all the time wait for the mixture to thicken

Do not boil the mixture or turn your back on it as it will turn into scrambled eggs!!!!!

Step 4
Allow to cool and then churn.

HONEYCOMB ICE CREAM

Use the recipe as above but leave out the vanilla pod.
Make your honeycomb.

1 cup castor sugar
4 tbs golden syrup
3 tsp bicarbonate of soda

Step 1
Using a heavy bottom pan heat the sugar and syrup. Once the sugar has dissolved put on a high heat for 5 mins.

Step 2
Take off the heat and add the bicarbonate of soda, and pour on to a greased tray. Allow to cool and break into bits.

Step 3
Churn your ice cream and add the honeycomb at the end. Freeze.

CHRISTMAS PUDDING ICE CREAM

Make your Ice Cream without the vanilla pod.

Add mince meat when you churn. I add about 8oz to a 1 litre mix.

CHOCOLATE FORT

This pudding is great to serve if you are having a dinner party – slightly retro but delicious

8oz plain chocolate
5 eggs
4oz caster sugar
4oz butter, melted
8oz savoy fingers
Strong black coffee
6.5in high sided, push out cake tin
4oz double cream to decorate

Step 1
Melt the chocolate and butter in a bowl over boiling water.

Step 2
Whilst the chocolate is melting, dip the Savoy fingers into the coffee and press them around the sides and then over the bottom of the greased cake tin. Because they are wet they will stick.

Step 3
Beat the egg whites until very stiff.

Step 4
Add the 5 egg yolks and caster sugar to the chocolate.

Step 5
Add the egg whites and amalgamate.
Pour in to the mould and chill for 24 hours.

Step 6
Push out and heap the top with the whipped double cream.
Chill again before serving.

Grate some chocolate on the top for garnish

CRÈME BRULÉE

600 ml double cream
9 egg yolks
zest of lime
8 tbs sugar
cinnamon

Step 1
Heat cream.

Step 2
Whisk egg yolks and sugar.
Add cinnamon and lime.

Step 3
Add the milk to the eggs and then whisk over a bain marie until the mixture thickens – about 10 mins. Be patient.

Step 4
Pour into your serving dish and chill.

To serve sprinkle with sugar and either use a blow torch to melt the sugar or put under a grill until the sugar has caramelised. Makes 8.

DANISH APPLE CAKE

This was one of our child hood favourites!! And incredibly easy.

8oz white breadcrumbs
3oz soft brown sugar
2oz butter
1.5lb eating apples
1tbs lemon juice
2oz caster sugar

Step 1
Mix together the breadcrumbs and brown sugar and cook in a heavy pan with the melted butter until crisp.

Step 2
Peel, core and slice the apples and cook to a pulp with the water, lemon juice and caster sugar.

Step 3
Arrange the apple mixture and crumbs in alternate layers in a glass bowl. You can decorate the top of the cake with whipped cream if you wish.

APPLE SLICE

This is a very easy apple pie and if you are not confident with pastry this is much simpler. It is in-between a cake and pastry.

For the pastry
8oz/225g self-raising flour
6oz/175g butter
2oz/50g castor sugar
1 large egg

For the filling
1lb/450g cooking apples i.e. Bramley's
3-4oz/75-100g castor sugar
½ level teaspoon ground cinnamon
1 tbsp raisins – optional

Step 1
Rub the butter into the flour until the mixture resembles coarse breadcrumbs.
Or use your mixer!!
Stir in the sugar and then mix to a dough with the egg.
Chill for 30 minutes, then roll out half the dough and line the bottom of the greased tin with it.

I bake this blind for 15 minutes, this is not absolutely necessary but I like my pastry crisper.

Step 2
On the top grate the peeled and cored apples, layering with the mixed sugar and cinnamon.
Add the raisins at this stage if you are using them.

Step 3
Roll out the remaining dough and place it on the top of the apple mixture.
Bake in a moderate oven – 180C/Gas Mark 4 for one hour.
Sprinkle with icing sugar, can be served hot or cold.

If you have apples ready prepared in your freezer you can use these instead of starting from fresh, just thaw, add sugar and cinnamon and place on the dough. You really do need to use Bramley's though as the tartness counteracts the sweet, cakey, pastry. Serves 10.

7. KATE'S "ABC OF WINE"

Having completed my BA (Hons) degree at University I spent some time in the world of fashion display fully intending to make my career in that world – until along came Caroline Mack!

Caroline had opened her first wine bar in 1985 in the City of London called "Punters" and, with my friend Mel, we got a part time job there -having returned from our round the world trip where we got as far as Jamaica, stayed for three months until we ran out of money and returned home!

At Punters I discovered the world of wine, the joys of Champagne and my future was set!

CAROLINE MACK & JEAN MARC CHARLES HEIDSIECK WITH KATE

In the next few years I ran wine bars in the crazy boom times for the City including my own bar in the City called The Mulberry Bush which the IRA only blew up twice!!

Having become fascinated by the world of wine and wanting to know more, I studied for my Certificate and Diploma of the Wine and Spirit Education Trust – the acknowledged route to Master of Wine.

Business got in the way and I did not complete the MW but I have always believed that whilst there are many great books on wine by certainly knowledgeable, talented and gifted tasters – Jancis Robertson and Michael Broadbent being amongst my favourites - I often searched unsuccessfully for a simple Tasting guide – and so I wrote one!!

It's called the ABC of wine and I hope you enjoy it!!

KATE IN THE WORLDS MOST EXPENSIVE VINEYARD – GRAND ECHEZEAUX – BURGUNDY OF COURSE!!!

The ABC of wine

A beginner's guide to wine appreciation

What is wine? Wine is an alcoholic beverage the result of the fermentation of grapes.

Wine is red, white or rose. Red wine comes from red grapes. White wine comes from white (and sometimes black!!) grapes. Rose wine comes from red grapes where the skins have been removed early in the process or where red wine is added to white wine. Rose champagne can also be a blend of red and white wine

All grapes have a 'pulp' centre which is white. (which is why you can make white wine from red grapes)

Fine wines cannot be made with poor grapes. Ripe good grapes will not produce good wine if the wine making processes is not carefully done. These two skills are viticulture and vinification. Wine is the fermented juice of the freshly gathered grapes.

Fermentation is a metabolic process resulting in chemical changes brought about by enzymes of micro organisms. Many types, both aerobic and anaerobic. Alcoholic fermentation is based on the transformation of sugar into ethanol and carbon dioxide.

So to summarise, fermentation is a natural process - as the freshly gathered grapes begin to warm in the summer heat the flora (yeast produces naturally on the skin of the grape) reacts with the sugars in the grape and the oxygen in the air and the grapes soon start to bubble away as the fermentation process begins.
Much heat is produced during fermentation and this is monitored and more often than not it is controlled.
Fermentation stops when all the sugar has been consumed by the yeast or the alcohol has risen to a level at which yeasts are killed.

Every process, method and technique used in the production of wine affects the taste of the end product in the bottle - whether this be the grape picking, the crushing, the pressing, the storage or the maturation.

The flavour of wine starts with the grape.
There are hundreds of different grape varieties all giving different flavours and textures to the end product, the wine. I will go into these in more detail later. So Let's start tasting!!

The sequence when tasting is:
LOOK, SMELL, TASTE

LOOK / APPEARANCE
Pour some wine into a glass- do not pour more than 1/3 in a glass.
Hold it by the stem and tilt it against a white background.
Look at the hue or wine at the rim.
If we have a white wine and it's almost green in colour it implies a young fresh wine, if its a deep honeyed yellow it implies a wine with age.
Red wines can go from a deep purple rim through garnet to a tawny / brown colour - indicating age.

SMELL
Pick up the glass, swirl the wine around to give it air and enable it to breathe and then put your nose over the glass and smell. All wine should smell clean and appetising.

An off odour that lasts for a few minutes after the wine has been opened is probably bottle stink and is just the consequence of being trapped in the bottle for some years.

If the wine smells corky or it smells of "mouldy wood" then the wine has probably reacted badly with the cork and it has tainted the wine. The wine will not get any better and should be discarded.

A straightforward fruity aroma will come from a young wine and a more complex bouquet from a developed wine.
Is it floral or spicy?
Is it light and ephemeral?
Is it intense and persistent?

Describe your initial reactions - always write down what describes the wine the best in your view.

TASTE
Take a good mouthful - push it around your mouth - over and under your tongue.
Notice how it tastes.
Notice the qualities of the wine - sweetness, acidity and tannin.
If it is a big mouthful - implies sweetness.
If the juices at the side of your mouth really start to run - implies marked acidity.
If the roof or your mouth dries or puckers - the wine contains considerable tannin.
(Spitting will enable you to taste more wines. When the alcohol goes into the blood stream it begins to numb your senses. There are no taste buds in the throat!!!!)

THE GRAPE VARIETIES
The white classics

CHARDONNAY

"The grower loves to grow it, the wine maker loves to fashion it, and we all love to drink it", the most popular grape variety grown in all the wine producing countries. Its home is in Burgundy (where it is the pre-dominant white grape variety) used in the Cote d'Or where it produces arguably the best wines in the world – The Puligny and Chassagne Montrachets, Meursault and Chablis.
But this grape variety has travelled far and wide and is quite happy to set down roots in a wide range of much warmer and cooler climates all over the world. It is a very easy grape to grow and vinify and produces high yields without compromising quality. Chardonnay does not have an overwhelming aromatic characteristic - its impact on the nose is broad and mute rather than sharp and piercing.

When young or from the cooler climates it tastes of fresh green apples or more exotic fruits of melon and pineapple in the warmer climates. With age the cooler climates acquire a rounded richness with buttery, nutty overtones. When coupled with oak (as it often is) it imparts toasty oak flavours and rich glacé fruit characters. New world Chardonnays by comparison to the old world are bigger and bolder with more redolent oak, alcohol and fruit.

RIESLING

This is a champion amongst grapes - although unfashionable, it has a distinctive style which changes throughout its development.
When young it has a racy acidity and an intense floral, lime or peach scented finesse. After a few years it turns into a rich petrolly mouthful.
This may sound revolting but those heady fumes are pure delight and when you get to smell one you will be totally amazed and entranced by the complexity and depth. Riesling adopts the country it is planted in and captures its character.

A Riesling from SE Australia is rich and full of fruit where you can almost taste the sun. In Germany it has a more steely character and slightly off dry. In Alsace it is normally vinified dry. Riesling is also susceptible to botrytis and so has an ability to make some of the world's best dessert wines.

SAUVIGNON BLANC

This is one of the most popular/ fashionable varieties of modern times, although not the greatest of justifications for claiming to be a classic variety! It produces dry refreshingly zesty and aggressively recognisable wines, ready to drink almost immediately, but it is not generally made for longevity.
Its purest styles are generally made in and around the Eastern Loire region with Sancerre and Pouilly Fume being the most distinguished. The classic aromas are of unripe green fruits and it is often described as "cats pee on a gooseberry bush".

In the best chalky /slatey vineyards the terroir comes through and is described as gunsmoke and flinty. Sauvignon grows best in the cooler regions of the world. It has achieved great notoriety in New Zealand and particularly the Marlborough region where Cloudy Bay is produced. Here it produces wines with a more tropical taste - often lychees. In warmer Australia the wine tends to be a little more rounded and can have greengage fruit.

SEMILLON

This variety is grown all over the world. "In most of these vineyards it sits around sullenly like an overweight schoolgirl. Showing awkward fatness or just plain dullness in the wines it produces. In odd places though, as if under the spell of a fairy godmother, it can be transformed into a raving beauty." Semillon is the predominant grape that produces world's greatest dessert wine - Sauternes. When young the wine is lemony and it responds well to ageing in oak where it attains a rich lanolin flavour described as wax with hints of orange. It can make heads turn in the Hunter valley in Australia for those who have discovered its charms there.

Other white varieties

GEWURZTRAMINER

This variety is distinctly perfumed and fragranced. It is often disliked by new wine drinkers for this reason. Words used to describe this wine vary from tropical fruits to highly perfumed flowers with lychees, roses, and cold cream all often mentioned. In Alsace it is a noble grape where it is generally vinified dry. It is also susceptible to noble rot and can produce wonderful "stickies".

VIOGNIER

This variety produces full bodied golden wines with an elusive bouquet of apricots, ripe pears and musky peaches. It produces some of the world's most expensive wines from the Rhone valley in France - Chateau Grillet and Condrieu. It is a difficult grape to grow and only produces low yields.

CHENIN BLANC

Its home is in the Loire valley where it can be dry, off dry, sparkling or sweet. Described as green apple and wax scented. It is planted extensively in South Africa.

The red classic varieties

CABERNET SAUVIGNON

This is a variety that has travelled the world and taken root in many countries. It is robust and easy to grow. It has a distinctive nose of blackcurrants and also a grassy herbaceous quality reminiscent of green pepper, green olives and eucalyptus. It is also very austere and high in tannins and for this reason it is usually blended with other varieties such as Merlot, Cabernet Franc and Shiraz. It has great ageing qualities and when aged in oak develops smoky, cedar scents. Its spiritual home is in Bordeaux where it is used to make some of the world's most famous and greatest wines, such as Chateaux Margaux, Latour, Lafite and Mouton Rothschild.

PINOT NOIR

Burgundy is the home of this temperamental yet delicious grape variety. It is probably the only area in the world where this grape consistently shines. It is a very difficult to grow and it mutates and degenerates at will and because of the small tightly packed bunches it suffers from rot and general fitness problems. The nose tends to be one dominated by strawberries and cherries, game, marmite and truffles.

MERLOT

This grape variety is far more amenable. It produces full ripe jammy flavours of fruits of the forest, plums and chocolate. It is normally blended (with Cabernet Franc) in Pomerol and St Emilion to make highly sought after wines such as Petrus and Chateau Ausone. The variety can be found throughout the world from Australia to Argentina.

KATE AT GEOFF MERRILLS WINERY OZ

SYRAH / SHIRAZ

Syrah's home is most definitely in the Rhone valley of France. Here it produces some of the world greats such as Hermitage and Cote Rotie. It is an easy grape variety to grow not suffering from large amounts of pests due to its thick skin and produces high yields without the loss of quality. The grape has wonderful tannins which help its ability to age. It is sometimes said to have flavours of burnt rubber, or smoke and tar. These are not exactly inspirational descriptives and we believe pepper, bitter chocolate and concentrated cassis are far better suited to describe this great varietal.

Other red Varieties

CABERNET FRANC

This variety is known as the lesser variety used in the blends of the great Bordeaux wines. It does however deserve more recognition than this and it is the grape primarily responsible for Chateau Cheval Blanc in St Emilion. The grape can be described as more herbaceous and is lower in tannin, acids, and extracts and can have aromas of raspberries, violets or pencil shavings. Cab Franc is grown in the Loire valley where it makes delicious rose as well as some of France's greatest, but little known reds.

GAMAY

This is the grape variety that is responsible for Beaujolais Nouveau!!!! The region even vinifies the grape in its own particular way known as maceration carbonique to specifically produce light wines with plenty of fruit for early consumption. It typically will be light purple with high acid, low tannin, and an aroma of inky fruit juice. The technique used often produces a smell of bubblegum.

GRENACHE

A hot climate variety which is used for blending more than it is used as a single varietal. However it is the dominant grape in Chateauneuf du Pape, its rounded style often masks the tannin content. It is grown widely in Spain and southern France. It is often used to make rosé.

NEBBIOLO

This grape variety has its home in NW Italy. It has a concentration of non fruity but complex bitter flavours which can be described as roses and tar and spice and a combination of extract, tannin and acidity that enables the wine to age. The peaks of this wine are reached in the production of Barolo and Barbaresco.

TEMPRANILLO

This is Spain's answer to Cabernet Sauvignon. It tends to be low in acidity and its flavour is often described as strawberries, spice and leather. It is often blended with other grape varieties. Used in Rioja.

SANGIOVESE

Widely planted in Italy and most famous in Tuscany. It gives rich, alcoholic and long lived wines, high in acidity and tannin. Chocolate and autumn berries.

7. DON'S "ART OF THE PARTY"

Having started the UK's first student marketing company in 1970 I was lucky enough to have the opportunity to work with some of the great creative companies in the exciting, newly developing, British music business.

Running events and promotions on campus led to regional disco and club promotions then artistes or PR launch parties. This led in 1978 to my formation of Broad Oak Vintners, latterly The Food & Drink Company, providing event management and catering – the first creative or theme catering company specialising in music and media. In the years to 1992 I had the privilege of running and catering some fantastic events.

HRH THE DUKE OF EDINBURGH

As news of our creative approach to catering for music events got around I was lucky enough to be chosen to run Royal Film Premier Parties for many great films. It was an honour to run the Royal Charity Premier Parties for Cubby Broccoli's James Bond films - A view to a Kill, The Living Daylights and Live and Let Die. I also ran other great premiers for films such as The Hunt for Red October, Crocodile Dundee, Batman and so many more.

Royal Film performances and parties led to my working with The Princes Trust and running Princes Trust receptions at Kensington Palace for TRH the Prince and Princess of Wales.

CUBBY BROCOLLY

I ran high security events at air shows through my old chum Nigel Rushman, the 50th Birthday party for the SAS given by HRH the Prince of Wales at Kensington Palace and the Prince of Wales 30th Birthday party in Birmingham with 3,000 young people from the Princes Trust!

Home and away I ran the backstage bar at "Live Aid" in London, parties in LA and New York, film festival parties in Cannes (Warner's 50th Birthday party) and more.

As the first licensee to get a license to sell beer to the 100,000 rock fans at the "Monsters of Rock" concert, I also ran many back stage and VIP areas for over 12 years at Donnington Park, Knebworth, Milton Keynes Bowl and, with my mobile Champagne bars, even Pavarotti by moonlight at Leeds Castle!

Having played briefly in bands in the late 60's I soon realised that I was not good enough to play guitar with the greats - but I did find out some years later that I could organise the events, catering and wines for them ... what joy!

I was lucky enough in my early years to work with some great people but I must especially thank Rita Pedley who stayed with me in difficult years and suffered long and hard as my PA and a great friend for so many years.

It was great to run events for such artistes as Led Zeppelin - with special thanks to The very Reverend Phil Carson of Atlantic Records in particular for Zeppelin at Knebworth 1978!! There were also parties for Phil Collins (ran his second wedding!) Queen, Rolling Stones, U2, David Bowie, Deep Purple, Paul McCartney, Simple Minds, Tina Turner, Police, Status Quo, Ronnie Wood and so many more.

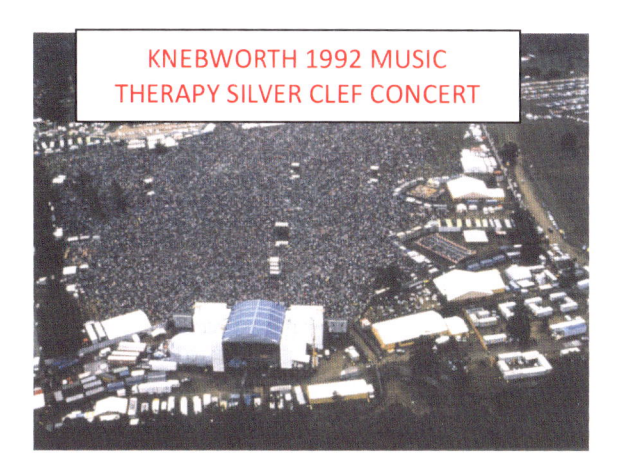

KNEBWORTH 1992 MUSIC THERAPY SILVER CLEF CONCERT

It was also great to work with the top managers and promoters – it is an absolute fact that the most successful artistes, without exception, have really good managers and promoters.

I enjoyed working with many of the greats including Harvey Goldsmith (not to forget Martin Goldsmith) Maurice Jones, John Giddings, the late Peter Grant, Bill Kirbishly and Tony Smith.

BRIAN BATCHELOR & TIM COCKING

Plus of course our clients (without whom...) especially Brian Batchelor, Des Brown, Chris Poole, Phil Symes and Carol Hayes.

Thank you all – it was fun!!

Throughout this period I developed and refined various checklists and systems for such events – in food and drink planning, checklists are everything!

DES BROWN & RON JOHNSON

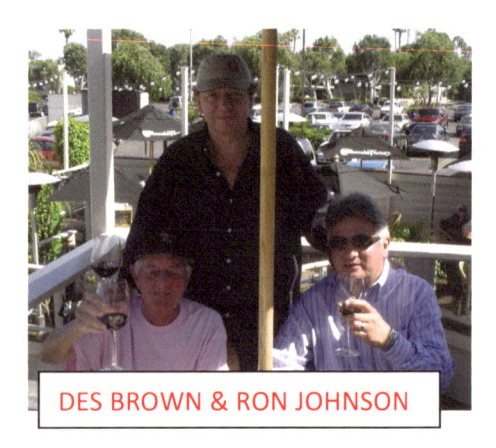

First, always, was the creative meeting! Some of you may laugh ... but this was a vital process that I always recommended ..... OK, often involving excellent lunches and (lots of) fine wines! Then it all came down to planning and budget!!!

ROYAL FILM PERFORMANCE KEN GREEN & SIR RICHARD ATTENBOROUGH

These rules apply today as they did then and in the same way if you are running an event for 10 people or 100,000!!

Take some time to work out what you really want and how you are going to do it – preferably over a glass of wine!

I call it "The Art of The Party" and for me it developed into five headline subjects that covered any and every event. I share this now in the hope that it may be of use to you in your event be it large or small!

The Art of the Party:

The five questions

What is it? party, reception, theme.
Where is it? venue, décor.
When is it? date, timings, start, finish.
Who is it for? – guest list, Invites.
Why? – understand why you are giving this event.

Get your five questions answered and then go deeper into the plan!

NIGEL RUSHMAN

Creativity – The Theme – Make it flow

Every great event has a start – middle – end. Make sure you have an idea of how the party will start then create the main event and finally how will it end... make a party flow and, if it's a big party, move.

We almost always, with big premier parties, ensured that the welcoming Champagne or drinks reception (if people are queuing for security or an entrance – give them a glass to keep them going!!) then led through to a main area and that in turn led to a smaller more intimate area that became the focus for the dancers, late bar and bacon sandwiches at the end!!

Once you have decided on your theme then you can have fun.

Lighting:

Whether it be the wedding party I ran at the National History Museum (above) or the garden party I organised for Robert Plants daughter's wedding (below) lighting can be everything. Whatever your event, always use simple candles and nightlights to light flowers. For example, an indoor dinner party can be transformed with up lighters on the trees in the garden – seen through the windows.

Décor:

I would always think of using flowers – but they don't have to be expensive or exotic.

Never underestimate the impact of candles with simple greenery and don't be afraid to jumble a few candlelit "props" on a table or in a corner – make it fun!

Probably the best example of this was when I ran Sir Richard Attenborough's "Cry Freedom" premier – an incredible film. The venue was on old London college and we used old bark and dead tree trunks, lit from behind by candles, to light the hall with an African choir singing in the background - it was spectacular!

Flowers:

I had the privilege of working with some of the great florists – particularly the magnificent Kenneth Turner.

It is impossible to beat the impact of flowers in a simple statement. Whether it be at home or in a big hall why not use wild flowers - we once dressed a massive room with cow parsley and it looked great or just use inexpensive or free (from the garden or hedge) greenery?

Sound:

Think this through for each of the three stages of the party, music can so often make or break a party. Change the mood and the music in different rooms!

Cutlery crockery and linen:

Table cloths do not have to be white and linen – the picture above is from a party I ran at The National Portrait Gallery. Cloths can be any colour and fabric!!

If you can, make the cutlery fun and the napkins interesting - it's amazing what a difference tying napkins with a few ribbons makes!

BACKSTAGE PASSES

Drinks:
This could, of course, be a whole series of books! What I hope I have done above is listed a few of the questions that may be of help and challenge your thinking – and of course refer to Kate's ABC of Wine and our chapter on Champagne!

When I was running events the main areas I tended to look at were:

Cocktails and welcoming drinks?
Champagne and Wines?
Beers?
Soft drinks?
Spirits? (don't forget all the mixers…)
Digestives?
Soft drinks – don't have to be boring!!

Food:
Hopefully the main part of our book will give you ideas for everything from small drinks party canapés though dinner parties to full blown events.

Apply the rules of The Art of The Party and you'll have a great (and enjoyable) time!

Operations:
For larger events you will need to look at all the other aspects that make a great event work including security, photography, video, production, printing and transport.

These aspects have to work together to make an event really flow (and when it works - then nobody knows what you did!) I worked with some of the best in the business in these areas and it was an investment that always paid off.

So remember the golden rule - Get in, run it, close it down, get out!

Budget!!
Always an interesting one and this applies if you are running the event or party for yourself or for someone else - don't forget the budget checklist.

Know what you intend to spend, allow for some extras and hopefully you will get no nasty surprises from bills at the end!!!

INVITES

I hope the above will give you a quick and easy guide as to maybe make your event flow and be less stressful for you the organiser!

At the end of the day it is all about timings

Timings:
It is corny but true – but really, really, really give yourself enough time - timing is everything!!!

Set out below a reduced version of my events checklist which I hope may be of help – spend time planning and you'll have a great event and, most importantly, you'll enjoy it as well!!

ART OF THE PARTY CHECKLIST

DATE:	
GUEST NUMBERS:	
TIMINGS: START	
FINISH	
LINEN	
CROCKERY / CUTLERY	
TABLES & CHAIRS	
LIGHTING	
CANDLES	
PHOTOGRAPHY	
MUSIC	
FLOWERS	
CAKE	
SERVING DISHES	
GLASSWARE	

TIMETABLE:	
SET UP	
EVENT START:	
SERVICE DRINKS	
SERVICE FOOD	
OTHER FOOD SERVICE	

OTHER THINGS HAPPENING e.g. FIREWORKS?	
RUBBISH REMOVAL: / CLEAR UP	

CHEF CHECKLIST

DISH	INGREDIENTS

DRINKS CHECKLIST

ICE	
WATER SPARKLING / STILL	
JUICES / SOFT DRINKS	
GARNISH	
WHITE WINE (S)	

RED WINE (S)	
WELCOMING DRINKS	
AFTER DINNER DRINKS	

FOOD SERVICE CHECKLIST

CANAPES / NIBBLES	
STARTERS	
FISH	
MAIN	
DESSERT / CHEESE	
SNACKS	
OTHER	

8. THE GREATEST AND OUR FAVOURITE – CHAMPAGNE!!

If we could only ever drink one wine again it would, without doubt, be Champagne! This glorious wine from one of the most northern wine areas in Europe has a breadth of styles and tastes that surpasses any other wine producing area.

We were both fortunate enough to be invited to attend "L'Academie du Champagne" – The Champagne Academy (Don in 1985 and Kate in 1995) a unique in depth educational course held annually for a lucky 16 selected students.

Founded in 1956, the course always takes place in the summer and the syllabus includes lectures by the Principals of the sixteen Member Houses covering all aspects of Grande Marques Champagne, with visits to vineyards, press houses, cellars, bottling plants and a cork manufacturer, as well as tutored tastings.

Each House shares in the instruction and entertainment of the course members during their stay, giving them the opportunity to meet the top management, winemakers and families of the sixteen Member Houses.

The course provides the most thorough grounding in the knowledge of a specific viticultural region of any wine producing area in the world.

All members sit an examination at the end of the course and on passing, receive the Champagne Academy's Diploma.

Over this unique course tastings are held morning and afternoon with fantastic gastronomic lunches and dinners accompanied by the greatest Champagnes of every style and vintage.

Both of us had the great honour of becoming "Chairman" of the Champagne Academy – Don in 1994 and Kate is Chairman this year – 2010.

In this chapter of our book we are not going to try and write a definitive book on Champagne – there are too many much better ones already!!

What we would like to do is to introduce you to some of our personal favourite Champagnes in a series of sections dedicated to the five main types of Champagnes as we view them.

Non Vintage
Special Cuvées
Rosé
Vintage
Prestige Cuvées

THE CHAMPAGNE ACADEMY CHAIRMAN 1994!

THE CHAMPAGNE ACADEMY CHAIRMAN 2010!

Non Vintage

Every House has its own, unique style and it is a manifestation of the wine makers talent in blending that creates, year after year, this same house style despite the weather and so many differing factors – from often up to 150 different still wines before the second fermentation – we've tried it and this is a seriously difficult job!!

In terms of styles the houses can be grouped according to their styles and the blend of grapes used. In the Grandes Marques only three grapes are used in Champagne – Chardonnay, Pinot Noir and Pinot Meunier.

The trick with non vintage Champagne is to try the different houses and see which one suits you! From the Chardonnay houses through to the Pinot Noir / Pinot Meunier and even aged in wood (such as Krug and Bollinger) they are all different and have their own styles – so go try them all and enjoy!!!

THE ORDRE DE COTEAUX DE CHAMPAGNE UK
CONSUL GENERAL JUSTIN LLEWELYN
THE AMBASSADOR – ROBERT POWELL
and the Consul for the South of England!!

Special Cuvées

These are Champagnes that are produced in smaller limited qualities – coming from a particular vineyard or made in a specific style. Each is unique.

If you are a fan of Pinot Noir you have to try Pommery's fabulous Blancs de Noir Wintertime – it's glorious, with fantastic depth and finish.

With its own Chateau and a vineyard set out in a chequer board of alternate White (Chardonnay) and Black (Pinot Noir) Vines, Taittinger's Les Folies de la Marqueterie is unique.

A particularly special blend of vintage Champagnes is Lanson's "Extra Age" Cuvée – launched to celebrate their 250th Anniversary - it is fantastic with Foie Gras!!!

Rosé

Ah, the joy of Rosé!!

The great family house of Laurent Perrier spearheaded the growth of Rosé with its wonderful Laurent Perrier Cuvée Rosé.

Driven by the family head, the mercurial (and sadly recently deceased – he will be much missed) Bernard de Nonancourt and created in 1968 this wonderful wine is made from the "savoir-faire" method - where the colour is obtained through the extraction of natural colour from the Pinot Noir grapes. Presented in an elegant bottle based on the old Champagne bottles of more than 200 years ago this iconic wine is just delicious!

Other great houses followed suit and amongst our favourite Rosé are the delicious Bollinger Rosé NV and Taittinge'rs Brut Reserve Rosé.

Vintage

Vintage Champagnes often offer the best value on a restaurant or wine merchants wine list – often not much more expensive than NV they offer fantastic style and elegance so look out for them and try them!

During a recent visit to Champagne and Pol Roger we had the joy of sitting with Hubert de Billy drinking a bottle of their Blancs de Blancs 1999 Vintage on the terrace of the Pol Roger gardens – it don't get much better!!

During Kate's year as Chairman of the Champagne Academy in 2010 we have also enjoyed Moet's unusually powerful 2003 vintage – from the hottest and earliest summer on record.

Earlier this year we enjoyed a bottle of 1985 Mumm – with Brough Guerny-Randall who was also with me on the 1985 Champagne Academy course – a great wine from a great year!

High point of this years Champagne Academy dinners was Laurent Perrier's Grand Siècle, which is probably Kate's favourite. Taittinger's Comptes de Champagne (blanc or rosé) is probably mine.

At this years Champagne Academy Past Chairman Dinner at The Ritz, we drank Magnums of Krug with Chef John Williams wonderful "Oeuf Fabergé" and it was one of the finest combinations we have ever tasted!

EXECUTIVE CHEF OF THE RITZ HOTEL JOHN WILLIAMS

Prestige Cuvées
Now this is where we can have fun!! From Moet's Dom Perignon early market leadership, through Louis Roederer's Cristal, Veuve Clicquot's Grand Dame and Pol Rogers Winston Churchill Cuvée, the Prestige Cuvee market has exploded and, for a treat, they just cannot be beaten!

Many people forget that the Champagne region is close and can be an easy trip for a long weekend or just a few days off. Go visit – it's worth it!!!

Many of the great Champagne houses welcome visitors and it is an area offering special gastronomic experiences!

From the magnificent restaurant "Les Crayers" in Reims, venue for the Champagne Academy course awards lunch every year and long time base of great Chef Gerard Boyer, to the lovely brasseries in Épernay and the many restaurants in the little villages of the Champagne region, we can think of little better than a few days visiting Champagne and driving through the vineyards, en route to another tasting or lunch!!!

Much has been written about "The Glory of Champagne" (to copy the title of our old mate Don Hewitson's book) and there are some wonderful quotes about it. To finish our brief snapshot into these magnificent wines, we leave you with two of our favourite quotes:

"I drink champagne when I'm happy and when I'm sad. Sometimes I drink it when I'm alone. When I have company I consider it obligatory. I trifle with it if I'm not hungry and drink it when I am. Otherwise I never touch it - unless I'm thirsty".
Madame Lilly Bollinger.

"Remember gentlemen, it's not just France we are fighting for, it's Champagne!"
Winston Churchill.

WITH SOME GREAT FRIENDS FROM CHAMPAGNE AT THIS YEARS CHAMPAGNE ACADEMY DINNER – VISCOUNT BERNARD DE LA GIRAUDIER, HIS SON OLIVIER DE LA GIRAUDIER, ALEXANDRA DE NONANCOURT AND JEAN BERCHON

9. CANAPÉS AND NIBBLES

BOUCHÉES

These are a great canapé but fiddly!! They are vol au vents and can be filled with anything.
You will need 2 pastry cutters 1 smaller than the other approx 3 cm wide and 2.7cm wide.
To Make 40 you will need 3 sheets of puff pastry.

Step 1
Line a tray with greased greaseproof paper.

Step 2
Use the cutter and cut 40 rounds and line then up on the greased greaseproof paper. Brush with a little milk.

Step 3
Cut another 40 rounds, and then with the smaller cutter cut the middle out. Put the pastry ring on top of the 40 already cut. Brush with milk.

Step 4
Repeat, but brush with egg yolk this time.

Step 5
Put in a moderate oven 4/5 gas and bake for 25 mins or until golden in colour.

With the little circle left over – I put on a little grated parmesan and bake. They are like cheese straws but little circles, and I hate to waste anything!!

BRUSCHETTA

Bruschetta is basically the Italian word for toast – or fried toast!!!! I make a range of bruschetta for parties and work on 2 pieces per person

Baguette or Ciabatta bread
Fresh herbs – sage, rosemary, basil?
Topping of choice
Olive oil

Step 1
Slice your baguette into rounds.

Step 2
Heat the frying pan. Add the olive oil and some fresh herb. The herb will flavour the oil. Gently fry the bread in the olive oil – leave to one side. They can keep for a few hours.

Step 3
Make any toppings and have them all ready – and then assemble at the last minute. Here are some suggestions that we like:

Goats cheese and basil – garnished with fresh basil
I cut the crust off the goats cheese and mix to a paste with finely chopped basil.

Prosciutto and olives
Put some prosciutto on the toast and garnish with olives chopped small.

Tomato, basil and olive oil
Cut the tomato into quarters and remove the pips. Cut the rest of the tomato into strips and then into little jewels of tomato. Mix with some olive oil and finely chopped basil.

Red pepper and blue cheese
I use tinned marinated peppers. Cut into small pieces. Put on the toast with a slice of blue cheese – put under the grill to melt.

Artichoke, parsley and lemon
Cut up the artichoke and mix with the parsley and lemon.

PRAWN COCKTAIL

Mini prawn cocktails – served either in a pastry case or in miniature shot glasses (don't forget small spoons if you do this!) are great!

Mix prawns with Marie Rose sauce.
Mayonnaise mixed with a little tomato ketchup and Worcester sauce.

CHEESE CROUTON – FOR SOUPS AND SALADS

Makes 6

1 Demi Baguette
Herb Leaves of choice
4 tbs Olive oil
6 tbs Parmesan grated

Step 1
Slice your bread.

Step 2
Fry the herbs in the oil to flavour the oil.

Step 3
Dip the bread in the oil.

Step 4
Press the grated cheese into the bread.

Step 5
Dry fry the crouton on both sides and serve.

Can be made in advance and reheated for 2 mins.

FISH GOUJONS

We make these for the "Fish N Chip" canapé that we serve in greaseproof cones. They are easy to make but I would suggest a deep fat fryer.

I fillet of cod
2 Cups of bread crumbs
2 eggs
Sunflower oil

Step 1
Slice the fillet of cod into stripes 4 cm long and ½ cm wide.

Step 2
Beat your eggs.

Step 3
Put the strips of fish into the eggs and then into the breadcrumbs so that the fish is completely covered.

Step 4
Put into the fridge till needed but for at least ½ hour.

Step 5
Get the fat to 200 – slightly higher that you would for fries. Cook your Goujons till golden. If you are making the fish and chips – keep the Goujons warm in the oven while you cook the chips. For presentation – put the chips into the base of the cone, with 2 or 3 Goujons on the top. Serve with tartar sauce or Heinz Tomato Ketchup!

MINI SCOTCH EGGS

These are great for a get together or picnic.

12 quails eggs
1 pack of good sausages – experiment with various flavours, but the classic is Cumberland.
Bread Crumbs
Oil for frying

Step 1
Hard boil the quails eggs for 3 minutes. Run under cold water to stop the cooking process.

Step 2
Peel the eggs.

Step 3
Split open the sausages from their skins and mix together.

Step 4
Take some sausage meat and flatten in the palm of your hand. Put 1 egg onto this and wrap the meat around the egg so that the egg is entirely covered.

Step 5
Roll the egg in the bread crumbs. Continue with the rest of the eggs.

Step 6
Get the oil good and hot – 200. Deep fry the eggs. This will take about 8 minutes.

Step 7
Allow to cool and serve.

PARMESAN CRISPS

These are fantastic with champagne!!!

Grate some parmesan – as much as you want.

Using a circular mould and a plastic cooking sheet, put a layer of grated cheese in the mould so you have a circular disc – continue until you have the desired quantity.

Cook in a hot oven gas 8 for 5 minutes.

Allow to cool briefly - serve.

PARMESAN BISCUITS

Equal quantities of flour and butter. For every 4oz of flour used, use 1oz of parmesan.

Put the flour and butter in a mixer or kitchen aid using the bread attachment.

When the mixture looks like bread crumbs – add the grated parmesan.

Continue the kitchen aid till a dough is formed.

Form the dough into sausage shapes and wrap in cling film and chill.

Cut the sausage dough into rings and put into a greaseproof paper lined tray and bake in a hot oven for 10mins.

ROAST MUSHROOM AND SAGE TARTS

I love using puff pastry and often have some left over and so have devised ways of using the pastry up!!! I love making these as they are quick and simple but look great.

18 small mushrooms
1 bunch sage
Sea salt and cracked pepper
Olive oil
Puff pastry
1 beaten egg

Step 1
Scatter the sage leaves into a roasting tray. Add the mushrooms but with there stalks up. Drizzle oil over and the S&P. Roast in a hot oven 200c gas 8 for 5 minutes.
Allow to cool.

Step 2
Put your pastry sheet onto a greased and paper lined baking tray. Using sharp knife cut into squares – depending on the size of your mushroom. Put 1 mushroom onto each square and then score around the mushroom. This allows the pastry to rise.

Step 3
Decoratively arrange the sage leaves onto the pastry. At this point they can be held in the fridge until you are ready to cook them.

Step 4
Liberally brush with egg,

Step 5
Bake in a hot oven 200c gas 8 for about 15 mins till risen and golden. Serve.

Other ideas
Tomato, olive and parmesan
Prosciutto and goats cheese

10. VEGETARIAN DISHES

DAUPHINOISE POTATOES

One of the easiest restaurant dishes to make. With this recipe I am not going to give precise ingredients.

Potatoes
Garlic bulb
Cream
S & P
Nutmeg

Step 1
Choose the baking dish you wish to use depending on how many people you are serving. I work on a medium sized potato per head.
Butter this dish.

Step 2
Using a mandolin slice the potatoes thinly.

Step 3
Take the garlic bulb, rub the casserole dish and rub over the sliced potatoes.

Step 4
Put the potatoes into the dish, layering with the cream, the salt and pepper and the nutmeg.

Step 5
Leave to sit for 10 mins to allow the cream to settle. Cover with foil and bake in the oven for 40 mins gas 5.

Serve immediately, or chill in the fridge and you can then cut shapes out of the dish and reheat.

FIG TARTE TATIN

I make this to go with lamb - preferably a rack or lamb cutlets. I have also made this for my vegetarian friends and serve it with any number of hot rice or vegetarian dishes

Like the Apple Tarte Tatin you will need 1 fig per person and pastry to fit on the top.

The dishes I use are approx 6 cm wide.

Put a layer of sugar into the dish and slice some butter on to this.

Cut the fig into quarters and place in the dish innards on the bottom.

Put in the oven for 40 minutes.

Put the pastry lid on the top and bake for another 30 minutes or until the pastry has cooked. Turn out and serve.

ROASTED PUMPKIN, BEAN AND COUS COUS SALAD

This is a great end of summer salad and fantastic with a BBQ.

2 cups Cous Cous
2.5 cups veg stock

700g roasted and caramelised pumpkin
200g blanched green beans / mange touts

3 tbs olive oil
½ tsp Harissa
¼ cup mint
1 tbsp honey
¼ cup lemon juice

Step 1
Roast your pumpkin.
Cut the skin off the pumpkin and cut into cubes about 2cm wide.

Put in a roasting tray and drizzle liberally with olive oil. Roast for 30 mins in a moderate oven.

Step 2
Allow the Cous Cous to soak up the veg stock.

Step 3
Add all the other ingredients and gently fold in.

Serve

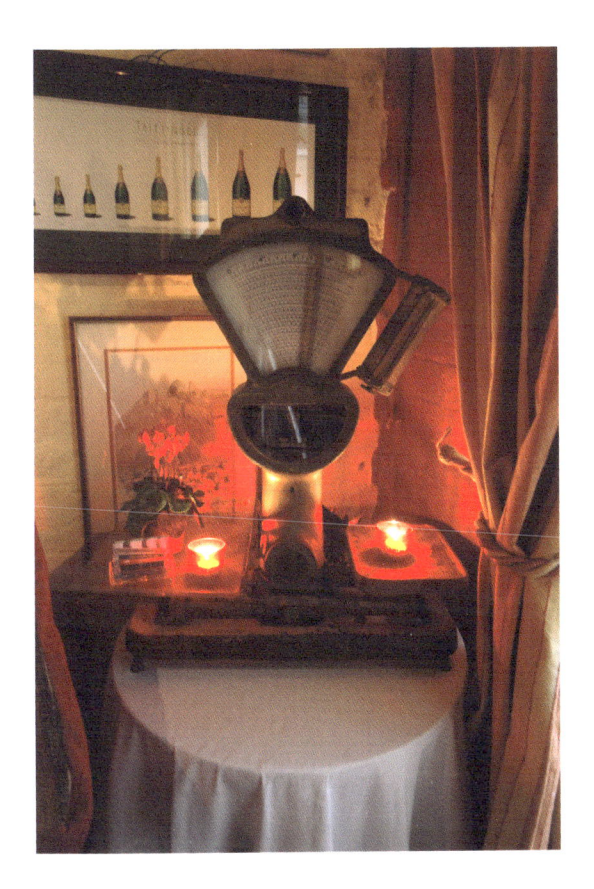

HOMEMADE CHIPS

There really is nothing better!

The trick to great homemade fries is to cook them 3 times.

So peel and slice your potatoes to your desired size – fat thin etc

If you have a deep fat fryer use this.

Let the oil heat up.

Put the chips in the pan and let them cook for 3 mins.

Take them out and let them rest for 5 mins.

Cook them again for another 3 mins and take them out and allow to rest. They should still be white but soft.

You can leave them at this stage for a couple of hours until you are ready.

Fry them for the third time. They should only take a couple of minutes to cook and brown.

POMMES PONT NEUF

These are really fat chips – cook as above then stacked three by three in a grid.

CHICKPEA PURÉE

1/ 2 Onion diced
1lb Dried Chick peas or 2 tins
½ tsp Cumin
½ tsp Paprika
100 g butter
juice 1 lemon
10ml white wine vinegar
Step 1

Soak your chickpeas in water. Enough water so they are just covered – approx ½ pint.

Step 2
Gently sauté the onion in a little olive oil until just browned.

Step 3
Add the cumin and paprika and cook for another minute.

Step 4
Add the soaked chickpeas and the water and cook for ½ hour.

Step 5
Whizz in your liquidizer – add the butter, lemon juice and vinegar.

Serve – with the calamari or as a dip.

This makes enough for dipping for a party of 12.

RED CABBAGE CASSEROLE

This is fabulous with Roast Pork or Duck. In the winter it is always on our menu.

1 Red Cabbage
2 White onions
2 Apples
Bay Leaves
2 tbsp Cider Vinegar
2 Tbsp orange juice

Step 1
Slice the red cabbage, as thin as possible.
Dice the onions small.
Peel and core and slice the apple.

Step 2
Layer the cabbage, onions and apple into a casserole dish.
Add the cider and juice.

Step 3
Seal the casserole dish and place in an oven for 1 hour on a moderate heat.

This is a very forgiving dish and can be cooked for longer etc. AS a kid I used to put this on at the same time as the Roast pork.

RICE 'N' PEAS

A great Jamaican dish that works with loads of mains but always with the Jerk Chicken.

1 cup Red dried pinto beans
2 cup rice
3 cup water
1 shallot
1 tbsp coconut milk
S&P

Step 1
Rehydrate your beans overnight in 3 cups of water.

Step 2
Change the water and cook the beans for 1 hour in another 3 cups of water.

Step 3
Drain the beans putting the water into a heavy bottomed pan.

Step 4
Rinse your rice and add to the pan with the diced shallot and the coconut milk.

Step 5
Put on the heat until the water is simmering. Turn right down and put a tight fitting lid on and cook for 10 mins.

If it starts to catch just turn the heat off – the rice will still cook.

After the 10 mins add the beans and stir. Put the lid back on and cook for a further 10 mins. You could put the rice in the oven if you wanted.

SPANISH POTATOES

This is a dish from my childhood and a dish we always served with roast leg of lamb. I have no idea why it is called Spanish potatoes – I have never seen this dish served in Spain!!

To serve 6 people
8 Large Potatoes
16 Rashers of streaky bacon
3 oz butter
1.5 oz flour
½ pint milk
S & P
4- 6 oz grated hard cheese

Step 1
Peel and boil/ steam the potatoes until cooked.

Step 2
While the potatoes are cooking, slice the rashers of bacon into bits and fry until crispy.

Step 3
Make a béchamel.
Melt the butter, stir in the flour and slowly add the milk. Add most of the cheese.

Step 3
Slice the potatoes about 1 cm thick.
Layer the potatoes with the bacon into an oven proof baking dish.
Pour over the béchamel and top off with the remaining cheese.

The dish can hold at this point until you are ready.

Step 4
Put under the grill for 10 minutes until browned and bubbling.
Serve.

STUFFING

When I have time, I try to breadcrumb all of the old bread and then allow to dry so that whenever we have a roast I can make stuffing. My favourite is sage and onion, which is below but experiment on the same principal. I have listed a few of my favourites.

3 cups breadcrumbs
1 large onion diced small
8 leaves sage chopped small
S & P
4 oz butter

Step 1
Sweat the onions in the butter until soft. Add the sage at the last moment to infuse into the onion.

Step 2
Add this to the breadcrumbs. Add S& P.

Step 3
Add egg to bind. If still a little dry add some milk or water.

Step 4
The stuffing needs to cook. I roll into foil and cook in a Bain Marie.

You could just put into a dish, cover with foil and pop in the oven with the roast.

Other ideas:
Mint and onion
Chestnut apricot and red onion
Rosemary and apple (I cook the apple till its soft and add to the breadcrumbs)
Thyme and pumpkin.

POTATO PURÉE

1 kg Potatoes – peeled
300 g Flour
2 eggs
S & P

Step 1
Cook the potatoes and then drain for 20 mins – so they are nice and dry.

Step 2
Add the flour and eggs and make into a dough.

ACKEE

When I travelled around Jamaica, I loved this unusual fruit that grows in the Caribbean. Traditionally this was served with salt cod. However I really dislike salt cod but have cooked this ever since without.

SO if you feel like trying something new!!!

1 tin ackee
4 tomatoes chopped finely
4 scallions/ shallots chopped finely
1 scotch bonnet chopped finely.
2 tbsp vegetable/ coconut oil

Step 1
Chop all your ingredients.

Step 2
Heat your oil in a pan and gently sauté the onions, scotch bonnet.
Add the tomatoes.

Step 3
Drain the ackee an gently rinse under cold water.

Add to the pot. Heat through and serve.

INDIAN SPICED RICE SALAD.

This is great hot or cold. When cooking rice always wash the rice to get rid of some of the starch, this will stop the rice sticking together. This dish involves steaming the rice and so you will need to have a tight fitting lid or use a foil cap.

To perfume the oil

1 cinnamon stick
4 cardamom pods
1 star anise
2 cloves
4 tbsp olive oil

250g Basmati rice washed
500ml water
1 tsp Cumin
1 tsp turmeric
1 tsp salt

To garnish
½ red onion
juice of 1 lime
baby spinach
small bunch coriander

Step 1
Perfume the oil. Using a heavy bottomed pot put the oil and the cinnamon stick, cardamom, star anise and cloves. Heat and when the room fills with the fragrant smell of the spices, remove the spices.

Step 2
Add the washed rice, cumin, turmeric and salt and stir. When the spices are mixed through add the water, bring to the boil and then turn the heat to low. Put the tight fitting lid on and leave for 10 mins. Take off the heat and leave for another 5 minutes.

Step 3
The rice should be lovely and fluffy.

If you want to serve this hot add the sliced red onion, spinach, lime and coriander and serve.

If you wish to serve this cold, spread the rice onto trays so that it can cool evenly.

Add the rest of the ingredients when you are ready to serve. Serves 6

PERRIN'S CORN PUDDING

I do this at thanksgiving!!

1lb creamed corn
4oz cornmeal
2 eggs
8fl oz milk
4oz melted margarine
1 tsp salt
2.5 tsp baking powder
A 2pint capacity ovenproof dish, approximately 2inches deep

Step 1
Pre heat the oven to Gas 4, or 350 degrees

Step 2
Grease the dish, then break the eggs into it and beat lightly with a fork.
To this add the corn, then the dry stuff, the milk and lastly the melted margarine. Mix.
Place in the oven for 40 minutes, after which time the pudding should be firm to the touch and slightly browned.

Great with roast chicken.

EXECUTIVE CHEF OF THE JUMEIRAH CARLTON TOWER SIMON YOUNG AND ALEXANDRA DE NONANCOURT

11. CAKES, BISCUITS, BREADS AND PIZZAS

CHOCOLATE CHIP COOKIES

This is my Auntie Ruth's recipe. She would make these for us every Christmas.

14 oz plain flour
2oz corn flour
14 oz margarine/ butter
2 eggs
8 oz castor sugar
1 tsp vanilla essence
6 oz milk chocolate (we always buy Cadburys family bar)

Step 1
Cream the sugar with the butter. Add the eggs, then the flours and essence.

Step 2
Using a knife break the chocolate into chips – we liked ours quite big.

Add to the mixture.

Step 3
Line a baking tray with baking paper and spoon the mixture in dollops onto the tray – depending on how big you want your cookies.

Step 4
Bake in the oven for 20 mins at 6.

COFFEE AND WALNUT CAKE

This cake keeps its moisture for days and so is good for a teatime treat for the whole week!!

4 eggs
2 heaped tsp instant coffee
8oz butter
8oz caster sugar
8 oz self raising flour
2 tsp baking powder

Filling and topping
2 0z butter
6 oz icing sugar
1 tbs coffee essence
1 tbs milk optional

Step 1
Grease 2 x 8" cake tins.

Step 2
Place eggs in a bowl and stir in the coffee till dissolved.

Step 3
Add remaining ingredients and beat until thoroughly blended.

Step 4
Divide mixture between the tins and level out. Bake for 25 minutes.

Step 5
Leave to cool and turn out.

Step 6
Butter cream
Blend together the butter, icing sugar, coffee essence and milk.

Spread half in the middle of the cake and the rest on top.

FRUIT SCONES

For 12 scones:
500g plain flour
1 tsp baking powder
1 tsp cream of tartar
Pinch of salt
100g butter
60g sugar
120g sultanas
½ pint of milk

Step 1
Sieve the flour, baking powder, cream of tartar and salt into a bowl.

Step 2
Add the butter cubed and rub in. You could use a machine to do this.

Step 3
Add the sugar and sultanas and mix.

Step 4
Add the milk and make dough.

Step 5
Turn out onto a floured board and roll out to 1cm deep. Cut into rounds whatever size you want.

This mix will make 12 scones 4cm in diameter.

Step 6
Cook in a moderate oven for 10 mins gas mark 6.

CHOCOLATE CAKE

200g chocolate
500ml milk
550g muscovado sugar
4 eggs
200 butter
350g plain flour
2 tsp baking powder
4 tbsp cocoa powder

Step 1
Melt the chocolate over a Bain Marie with half the milk and half the sugar.

Step 2
Cream the butter with the remaining sugar. Whisk in the eggs.

Step 3
Add the sieved flour, cocoa and baking powder, in 3 batches. Do this gently using a spoon.

Step 4
Add the chocolate and the remaining milk.

Step 5
Divide the mixture between 2 x 8" cake tins and bake in a moderate oven gas 3 160c for about 25 minutes.

Allow to cool and fill and cover with the chocolate ganache.

CHOCOLATE GANACHE

220g dark chocolate
2mm ml double cream

This is so easy to make and soooo delicious. Melt the chocolate over a Bain Marie, add the cream and stir till rich and glossy!!

KENTUCKY GINGERBREAD

3 eggs
8oz sugar
8oz molasses/black treacle
8oz margarine, melted
1tsp ground cloves
1tsp ground ginger
1tsp cinnamon
1lb self raising flour
8 fl oz boiling water

Step 1
Pre heat the oven to 350F or gas mark 4, and grease an oblong tin 13" by 9.5" by 2".

Step 2
Mix the eggs, sugar, molasses, margarine and spices in a large mixing bowl and beat the mixture until it forms a smooth batter.

Step 3
Gradually add in the flour and then add the boiling water, which will make the cake mixture very thin. To prevent the mixture from becoming lumpy, it is sometimes better to add the water and flour alternately.

Step 4
Pour this into the cake tin and bake for about 45 minutes or until the top springs back when lightly touched in the centre.
When you remove the cake from the oven sprinkle it with granulated sugar unless you intend to cover it with the fudge icing below.

FUDGE ICING

8oz icing sugar sieved
2oz margarine
2tbs milk

Warm the margarine and milk, but do not let them boil.
Add the sugar to the milk and leave to cool before spreading on the gingerbread.

VICTORIA SPONGE CAKE

I often make a cake as a birthday present for someone and they are so easy. All you have to remember is equal quantities of each ingredient. So if I wanted to make a mini cake I would just use 1 egg and then 2oz of flour sugar and butter!!

The quantities here will make a cake for a 7/8" cake tin.

250g self raise flour
250g sugar
250g butter
2 tsp baking powder
4 eggs

Step 1
Cream the butter and sugar.

Step 2
Add the eggs, the sieved flour, baking powder and beat.

Step 3
Using 2 x 8" cake tins greased, split the mixture equally and then bake in a moderate oven gas 6 for 30 mins.

Step 4
Allow to cool.

Assemble your cake with butter cream and icing.

PIZZA

Everyone loves pizza. It really is very easy to make pizza dough and you can then choose your own toppings. Let your imagination go!! Never forget that freshly made mini-pizzas are one of the world's best canapés!!

BASIC PIZZA DOUGH

1 sachet dried yeast
150 ml 5 fl oz warm water
2 teaspoons honey
300g / 11oz flour
½ tsp salt
45ml / 3 tablespoons olive oil

Step 1
Dissolve the yeast in the warm water with the honey and leave for 10 minutes until it starts to froth.

Step 2
Put the flour, salt and olive oil into a bowl. Add the yeast solution and stir until the ingredients come together.

Step 3
Kneads the dough on a lightly floured surface till smooth.

Step 4
Lightly oil a bowl and put the dough in the bowl and cover with cling film.

Leave in warm place. It should double in size fairly quickly (30min to an hour). Knock it back (just punch the dough so it deflates).
Let rise again, knock back.

You can now use the dough when you want.
I like to make the dough in the morning so that it is ready for when I need it, later in the day. It will also keep in the fridge for 24 hours at this stage.

I like my pizza rustic and fairly thin. This dough should make 4 good sized pizzas.

Step 5
Divide the dough into 4.

Step 6
Roughly roll the dough out in a circle and add your toppings.

Step 7
Place the pizza on a greased baking tray and in the hottest oven possible bake for 7-10 mins

My favourites: Passata / thinly sliced red onion and blue cheese / Chinese Duck Hoi Sin, cucumber and spring onion / bean sprouts and mozzarella

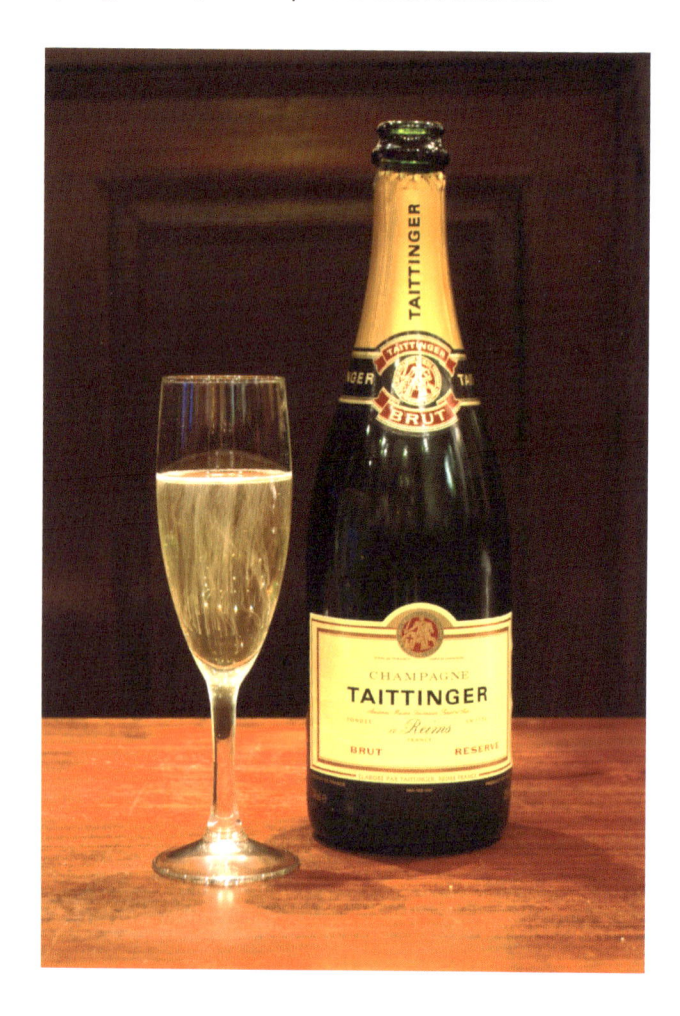

FOCACCIA

I have always had a problem with baking bread – but found Focaccia the easiest thing ever!!

1 packet dry yeast
280ml 9.5 fl oz warm water
60ml 2 fl oz white wine
600g 1 1/4lb flour
2 tsp salt
2 tbs olive oil
Salt crystals plus any other garnish you fancy – onions, rosemary tomato etc

Step 1
Add the yeast to the warm water and wine and leave for 15minute to bubble.

Step 2
Sieve the flour into a large bowl and add the salt. Make a well in the centre and add the yeast solution. Mix with a fork till it comes together and then add the oil and using your hands bring together to a lump of dough.

Step 3
Turn this out onto a floured board and knead for 5 – 10 minutes until the dough is smooth. The dough will be moist.

Step 4
Leave in an oiled bowl (cling film the bowl) in a warmish place to rise.

Step 5
Turn onto a floured surface and roll into the shape you desire.

Put onto greased tray. Use your fingers to imprint dimples into the dough. Cover again with Clingfilm and leave for 2 hours.

Step 6
Use the salt and any other decoration on the top of the bread and drizzle with some olive oil

Bake for 25 mins in a hot oven gas 8 230c

5 MINUTE FOCCACIA

1lb flour
1 sachet yeast
125 ml oil
½ pint warm water

Put the flour, yeast and oil together.
Slowly add the warm water.
Grease a baking tray and spread dough on to it.
Add sea salt or rosemary if desired.
Cover with damp cloth and leave for 30 minutes.
Cook for 20 minutes Gas 6.
Add oil half way through.

12. DRESSINGS, SAUCES, STOCKS AND JAM

BREAD SAUCE

A favourite for game birds and the Christmas turkey.

1 small onion
4 cloves
½ pint milk
3 cups breadcrumbs

Step 1
Spike an onion with 4 cloves.

Step 2
Put the onion in the milk and bring to the boil.

Step 3
Add the milk to the breadcrumbs – season with S & P and nutmeg.

Step 4
Return to the heat until the desired consistency is achieved. About 2 mins.

BURGER RELISH

I love burger relish and have devised this one – I will always make it and it only takes a few minutes.

1 shallot
4 cornichons
½ tin chopped tomatoes
S & P

Step 1
Dice your onion and sweat gently in a little olive oil.

Step 2
Add the tinned tomatoes, the cornichons chopped very small and seasoning. Allow to cool and let the flavours mingle. Serve!!

COCONUT DRESSING

½ cup coconut cream
2 tbs lime juice
1 tbs fish sauce

CRANBERRY AND ROAST SHALLOT CHUTNEY

I love making a few jars of this for Christmas time – perfect for the Turkey or any other cold cuts of meat or pates.

1lb Shallot
3 tbs Olive Oil
8oz Soft Brown Sugar
S & P
1lb Cranberries
1 inch Root Ginger
1 tbs Mustard Seed
¼ Pint Red Wine
3 Tbsp Crème Cassis

THE CONTENTED VINE

Step 1
Plunge shallots in boiling water for 5 minutes to loosen skins.

Step 2
Remove skins.

Step 3
Halve shallots lengthways and roast with olive oil and 3 tbsp of sugar. Season with S&P.

Step 4
In a saucepan put the grated ginger, remaining sugar, mustard, red wine and vinegar and cranberries.
Simmer for 10 – 15 minutes.

Step 5
Stir in shallots. Deglaze roasting tin with cassis and reduce to a syrup.

Step 6
Add to cranberries and simmer again for 10 – 15 minutes until thick.

Store in air tight jar.

CRANBERRY, PORT AND ORANGE RELISH

250gm 9oz fresh cranberries
120ml 4 fl oz port
Juice 2 oranges
75gm 3oz light brown soft sugar
½ tsp cinnamon
Freshly grated nutmeg

Step 1
Put the port, orange juice, sugar and cinnamon into a saucepan and heat gently till the sugar has dissolved.

Step 2
Bring to the boil and add the cranberries.

Step 3
Lower the heat and cook till the cranberries begin to pop and the relish becomes thick and jammy. Grate in the fresh nutmeg. Store in jars.

HOLLANDAISE SAUCE

This is easier than you think and is the perfect accompaniment for poached salmon and is, of course, one of the ingredients for Eggs Benedict.

2 egg yolks
4 oz melted butter
splash of lemon juice
Splash of water.

Step 1
Put a pan of water on to boil.

Step 2
In a bowl that will sit on top of the water pan, put your egg yolks in.

Step 3
Add a dash of lemon juice and a tsp of water. Whisk.

Step 4
Turn the water pan down to a simmer and put your eggs on top of this and whisk. The eggs will slowly cook. But keep whisking about 3 mins.

Step 5
Take of the water and slowly add the melted butter, while you whisk. As if by magic it will start to thicken and "voila" Hollandaise!!. This will make about a cup full.

PRESERVED LEMONS

These are used in many Mediterranean dishes and dips. I always like to have a jar available and will add them finely chopped up into salads, casseroles etc.

250 gm coarse salt
10 lemons scrubbed and quartered (unwaxed)
1 bay leaf
2 – 3 cloves
1 stick cinnamon

Step 1
Sterilise jar and scatter a handful of salt in jar.

Step 2
Put lemons in a bowl with remaining salt and rub vigorously.

Step 3
Pack in jar with the lemons turned inside out inserting the bay leaf, cloves and cinnamon stick.

Step 4
Press down hard to release as much juice as possible.

Step 5
Cover with extra juice.
Cap tightly and mature for at least a month.

QUICK CHICKEN STOCK

1 Chicken Carcass
1 Onion
2 bay leaves
Water

Step 1
Put the chicken carcass in a pot with the onion cut in half lengthways and with the skin on. Add the bay leaves and cover with water. Approx 3 pints.

Step 2
Bring to the boil and then simmer for 40 minutes.

Step 3
Strain and cool.

I will often serve this with a few noodles thrown in as chicken noodle soup!!

LAMB OR BEEF STOCK

The CV stock pot was constantly on the go and was the base for all of our jus. Use beef or lamb bones depending on the dish you want to use the stock for. Your local butcher will let you have bones - sometimes for free or for a small charge. They will always charge you for veal bones. Chefs use veal bones as the marrow in them is better.

3lb bones
1 bottle red wine
2 onions
1\2 head of celery
2 carrots
A handful of parsley & 4 bay leaves.
Water
3 tbs Tomato paste

Step 1
Put the bones into a roasting tray and put in the oven for 30 minutes to roast on gas 5.

Step 2
Mix the paste with a little water and spread over the bones and roast for another 20 mins.

Step 3
Put all the veg and herbs into a large pan - just chop the onion in half leaving the skin on.

Step 4
Add the bones from the oven and pour in the red wine. Pour in enough water to cover the bones and veg approx 3 pints.

Bring to the boil and then turn down to a simmer. Do not boil as the stock will be cloudy. With the tray that the bones were roasting in pour some water onto this and scrape all the bits then add to the pot.

Simmer for 4 hours, skimming when necessary to take away the excess fat.

Step 5
Strain the stock.

Step 6
Demi glace is when we reduce this stock by half so it becomes rich. When we want to use this for a dish we reheat and add a knob of butter.

SWEET CORN RELISH

This is so simple to make and perfect for the burgers.

1 tin sweet corn drained
1 tomato chopped
1 tbs sugar

Heat until there is no liquid left and slightly sticky but do not let it catch and burn!!

TARTAR SAUCE

1 cup Mayonnaise
20 Chopped capers
Splash Lemon juice
1 tsp Chopped Parsley

Put all the ingredients into a bowl and mix.

VEGETABLE STOCK

2 onions
1 leek
2 carrots
½ celery head
1 handful of big leaf spinach
1 handful of pea shells if available otherwise frozen peas.
6 bay leaves
s & p

Step 1
Cut your onions in half lengthways keep the skin on.
Put in a large pot with the other vegetables except the spinach and peas. Add the bay leaves and s& p

Step 2
Cover with water – about 3 pints and bring to the boil.

Step 3
Simmer for about 20 mins. Skim if necessary. Don't boil as this will make the stock cloudy.

Step 4
Add the spinach and peas and simmer for another 20 mins.

Step 5
Strain and cool.

I freeze my stock in ice cube containers so that I have stock available when I want it.

JERK MARINADE

I love this marinade for either chicken or pork. You can cheat and buy a jar from the supermarket, but I find its always better to make your own and then you can taper the spices to your personal requirements.

The core ingredients are scallions, thyme, allspice, ginger, scotch bonnet peppers, black pepper, nutmeg and cinnamon. Basically grind the spices in a pestle and mortar and then add the rest of the ingredients. Use is lavishly over the chicken/ pork and marinade for at least 4 hours.

Cook the pork for up to 4 hours – I would be inclined to use belly pork. If you wanted to bbq the pork I slow roast for 2 hours in the oven first and then grill on the BBQ.

BBQ the chicken slowly for 40 mins turning constantly. Or bake in the oven for 40 min and then finish under the grill for 10 mins.

MY JERK RECIPE

8 sprigs thyme, finely chopped
8 scallions or shallots, chopped finely
1 cm piece of fresh ginger finely chopped or grated.
1 scotch bonnet, deseeded and chopped (more if you want the marinade hotter)
1 clove garlic, chopped
1 teaspoon ground allspice
¼ tsp ground nutmeg
1 tsp ground pepper
1tsp ground coriander
¼ tsp cinnamon
juice of 1 lime
4 tbsp olive oil

STRAWBERRY JAM

I love making jam – it is so simple and you have the pleasure of jam for the whole of the winter.
This will make 8 jars of jam.

4lb Strawberry
4lb sugar

Step 1
Hull and wash the strawberries.

Step 2
Add the sugar to the strawberries and leave to sit for an hour or overnight.

Step 3
Heat the strawberries and allow to simmer until jam setting point is reached.

Step 4
Allow to cool and put into sterilized jars.

RINDLESS LEMON MARMALADE

We make this recipe to serve with our spit roasted chicken. It works just as well when roasting a chicken - halfway through the cooking smear a tablespoon on the chicken and continue roasting. You can also just spread it on toast! The same recipe can be used for Seville oranges. I love the tangy taste of marmalade but never liked the 'bits'. So if you are like me this recipe is perfect for you.

1lb unwaxed lemons
Pectin sugar
3 pints of water
Muslin cloth
Jam kettle or large saucepan

Step 1
Cut the fruit in half and squeeze the juice out into a saucepan.

Step 2
Put the pips and lemons into the muslin and tie up into a bag and put in the saucepan with the juice.

Step 3
Add the water and soak for a minimum of 3 hours, preferably over night.

Step 4
Bring to the boil and simmer for approx one hour.

Step 5
Take the bag out squeezing out as much juice as possible.

Step 6
Add the sugar; bring back to the boil until you reach setting point. This should be fairly quick – 20 mins.

APRICOT JAM

1 ½ lb ripe apricots
1 lb granulated sugar

Step 1
Wash your apricots and half and quarter and place in your jam kettle.

Step 2
Break the nut and take out the soft white center – smells just like almonds!!
Chop these and add to the pot.

Step 3
Add the sugar.

Step 4
Heat until you reach setting point on your thermometer. This will take about 30 mins depending on the sweetness of your apricots.

Bottle in sterilized jars.

There is a lot of pectin in apricots so normal sugar is fine to use.

13. MENUS & WINE LIST

Wine list October 2010

THE CONTENTED VINE

WHITE WINES

FRANCE

SOUTHERN FRANCE & RHONE
Chardonnay Terres du Sud VDP d'Oc 09	15.50
La Comtesse Vdp D'Oc 09 (Sauvignon Blend)	15.50
Sauvignon Bergerie de la Bastide VDP d'Oc 09	16.50
Guigal Cotes du Rhone 09	24.00

LOIRE
Sauvignon Touraine Guy Allion 09	20.50
Sancerre Dom Pascal & Nicolas Reverdy 08	33.00
Pouilly Fumé Villa Paulus Masson Blondelet 07	39.00

BURGUNDY
Macon Uchizy Domaine Talmard 07	28.75
Bourgogne Chardonnay Dom Monnier 06	29.75
Chablis Premier Cru Vaucopin Gilbert Picq 07	32.85
Clos du Chateau de Puligny-Montrachet 06	38.95
Saint-Romain, Deux Montille 06	45.25
Chassagne-Montrachet 1er Cru 06, Dom Bernard Moreau et fils	61.50

GERMANY & ALSACE
Riesling Deinhard Classic 08	19.00
Gentil Hugel 08	24.50
Riesling Spaetlese Graacher Himmelreich 04 Friedrich Wilhelm Gymnasium	34.85

ITALY & SICILY
Inzolia Vini del Sole Sicily 08	16.95
Pinot Grigio Trefilli 09	18.00
Verdicchio Serra del Conte 08 DOC	18.00
Felanghina beneventamo 08 IGT	20.00
Rorera Arnels Coschina Pellerino DOCG 06	20.00
Dogajolo Carpineto Toscano 09	22.00

SPAIN & PORTUGAL
Ademas Viura 08	15.50
Don Cristobel Castilla y leon 09	16.50
Macabeo Kalius Bodega Monfil Carinena 08	16.95
Vina Esmereida Torres 09	19.50
Alba de Miros Verdejo Rueda 09	25.00
Albarino La Val Rias Baixas DO 08	28.75

AUSTRALIA & NEW ZEALAND
Chardonnay Tyrells Old Winery 08 Hunter Valley Maclaren Vale	21.00
Verdelho Old Winery Tyrells 08	22.00
Sauvignon Blanc Bishops Leap Marlborough NZ 08	24.75
Chardonnay Xanadu Margaret River 08	29.00

ROSÉ WINES
Syrah Grenache Rosé Sixieme Sens Bertrand VDP d'Oc 09	18.00
Château de L'Aumerade Cuvée Marie Christine Cotes de Provence Rosé AC 09	24.00
Whispering Angel Chateau d'Esclans Provence Rosé 07	41.00

WINES BY THE GLASS

	125ml
Champagne Taittinger Brut Reserve	9.00

WHITE — 175ml
Chardonnay Terres du Sud VDP d'Oc 09	4.00
La Comtesse Vdp D'Oc 09 (Sauvignon Blend)	4.00
Pinot Grigio Trefilli 09	4.75
Vina Esmereida Torres 09	5.00
Riesling P Lehmann Eden Valley Barossa Oz 08	5.25
Chardonnay Tyrells Old Winery 08	5.50
Guigal Cotes du Rhone 09	6.00
Gentil Hugel 08	6.50
Sancerre Dom Pascal & Nicolas Reverdy 06	8.50
Chablis Premier Cru Vosgros Gilbert Picq 07	8.50

ROSÉ
Syrah Grenache Rosé Sixieme Sens Bertrand VDP d'Oc 08	5.00

RED
Syrah / Grenache Terres du Sud VDP d'Oc 09	4.00
Merlot Le Marquis 09	4.00
Coronas Torres 05	5.25
Château Verriere Bordeaux 07	5.75
Pinot Noir Tyrells Old Winery 09	5.50
Cotes du Rhone Guigal 09	6.25
Côtes du Rhône Bouquet des Garrigues Le Clos du Caillou 06	9.50

CHAMPAGNE

CHAMPAGNE TAITTINGER
One of the last great family Champagne houses

	Glass	Bottle
TAITTINGER BRUT RESERVE NV	9.00	43.25
TAITTINGER Les Folies de la Marquetterie		67.50

OTHER GRANDE MARQUES
LAURENT PERRIER Brut L-P	49.50
VEUVE CLICQUOT Yellow Label Brut	49.50
POL ROGER Brut Réserve NV	49.50
POMMERY NV	45.00
BOLLINGER Special Cuvee	55.00
LAURENT PERRIER Ultra Brut	59.00

ROSE CHAMPAGNE
BOLLINGER ROSE	65.00
LAURENT PERRIER	65.00

VINTAGE CUVÉES
LAURENT PERRIER 1999	63.50

PRESTIGE CUVÉES
Cuvee LOUISE POMMERY 09	105.00
Dom RUINART Blanc de Blancs 93	165.00
TAITTINGER Comtes de Champagne Blanc de Blancs 95	165.00

DESSERT WINES Glass or Half Bottle
	100ml	375ml
Raisined Semillon Beelgara 08 Riverina NSW Oz	4.90	15.00
Sauternes Petite Vedrine 05	8.95	29.00
Pedro Ximenez Cardenal Cisneros	8.50	

www.contentedvine.com

RED WINES

FRANCE

SOUTHERN FRANCE
Syrah / Grenache Terres du Sud VDP d'Oc 08	15.50
Merlot Le Marquis 09	15.50
Merlot Dom Nordoc VDP d'Oc 08	16.95
Pinot Noir La Boussole VDP Méditerranée 08	23.75

RHONE
Cotes du Rhone Guigal 09	25.75
Côtes du Rhône D'Alary 08	25.75
Coteaux Du Languedoc Les Combes Rostaing 06	28.75
Dom de Mourchon Seguret Cotes du Rhone Villages 07	36.00
St Joseph Andre Perret 08	36.00
Côtes du Rhône Bouquet des Garrigues Le Clos du Caillou 06	36.00
Gigondas Guigal 06	37.00
Gigondas Chapoutier 07	37.50

BURGUNDY
Marsannay Sylvain Pataille 05	41.50
Chassagne 1er cru Maltroye 01	57.50
Chambolle-Musigny Les Babillères Deux Montille 06	65.75
Volnay Taillepieds Voilenay Angerville 01	76.00
Aloxe Corton Les Morais Michel Saban 05	77.50
Nuits Saint Georges 1er Cru Les Damodes Michel Saban 05	82.50

BORDEAUX
Château Verriere, Bordeaux 04	22.00
Haut Medoc Cht Semonlon 07	32.00
Chateau de Fontbal Grand Cru St Emillion 04	39.50
Chateau Teyssier Grand Cru St Emilion 05	39.50
Le Dome Grand Cru St Emilion 04	49.50
Brio de Chateau Cantenac Brown Margaux 04 2nd wine Chateau Cantenac Brown 3rd Growth	54.50

ITALY
Carazita Rosso Irpinia Tenuta Ponte 03	19.00
Dogajolo Toscano Carpineto 07	22.00
Toscano Rosso, Ciacci Piccolomini 07	26.50
Chianti Classico Carpineto 06	40.00

SPAIN & PORTUGAL
El Tidon Tempranillo/Cabernet Ondarre 08	16.50
Don Cristobal Tempranillo Castilla y Leon 07	16.50
Kalius Tinto Garnacha 08	16.95
Coronas Torres 05	20.00

THE AMERICAS
Cabernet Sauvignon Riojanas Argentina 08	16.50

AUSTRALIA & NEW ZEALAND
Cabernet Sauvignon Tyrells Lost Block 05	17.50
Merlot Foundstone Riverland SE Oz 07	18.00
Grenache Barossa "Art Series" Peter Lehmann Oz 06	19.50
Shiraz Barossa Weighbridge Peter Lehman 08	19.50
Pinot Noir Tyrells Old Winery 09 SE Oz	21.00

October 1998

THE CONTENTED VINE
17 Sussex Street, Pimlico Village, London SW1. Tel 0171 834 0044

SANDWICHES

Roast Chicken and Warm Crispy Bacon Club	3.95
Honey Roast Ham & Emmenthal Club	3.95
Minute Steak Baguette with Onion Marmalade served with Fries	6.95
Marinated Chargrilled Peppers with Pesto Mayonnaise in a Baguette	4.95
Smoked Salmon	4.95

BAR SNACKS

Cocktail Sausages with a Mustard Dip	2.75
Potato Skins with Sour Cream and Tomato Salsa	2.25
Mini Chevre Tartlets with Caramelised Onions	2.25

TEAS, COFFEE and JUICES

Espresso	1.30
Double Espresso	1.85
Cappuccino	1.85
A Pot of Caffetiere Coffee	1.50
A pot of De Caffeinated Coffee	1.50
Selection of Twining Teas	1.25
Hot Chocolate	2.00
Freshly Squeezed Orange Juice	1.60
Spiced Tomato Juice	1.60
Fresh Squeezed Still Lemonade	1.60

FROM OUR TRADITIONAL SPIT ROAST

Spit Roast Chicken with Green Salad and French Fries	7.95
THURSDAY & FRIDAY : English Spit Roast Duck	9.95

STARTERS

Baked Five Onion Soup with a Parmesan Crouton	3.95
Baby Beetroot and Quails Egg salad	3.95
Herb Leaf and Rocket Salad, Shaved Parmesan & Caesar Dressing	3.95
Leek & Courgette Tartlet with Rocket Balsamic Salad	4.25
Scottish Smoked Salmon	4.75

LARGE PLATES

Chargrilled China Sea Escolar Fish, New Potatoes & Coriander Butter	8.95
Glenbervie Steak Hache with Green Salad & Fries	8.95
Grilled Polenta with Mediterranean Vegetables, Parmesan Shavings on a Pesto Sauce	7.95
Stir Fry Vegetables with Black Bean Sauce & Chinese Yellow Noodles	7.95
With Chicken	8.95
Home-made Herb and Ricotta Ravioli with a Tomato & Basil sauce	7.95
Loz's Glenbervie Beef and Coriander Burger with Relish and French Fries	7.95
Grilled GLENBERVIE Sirloin Steak with Rotisserie Baked Potato and Green Beans	14.75

DAILY SPECIALS

Monday
Roast Pork with Apple Sauce, and Spring Greens and Mash   8.95

Tuesday
Glenbervie Beef Sausages with Horseradish Mash and Onion Gravy   7.95

Wednesday
Steak and Kidney Pie with Buttered Potatoes and Cabbage   8.95

Thursday
Braised Lamb Shank with Mash & Seasonal Vegetables   8.95

Friday
Beer Battered Fried Cod with Chips and Mushy Peas   8.95

Saturday and Sunday
BRUNCH MENU ALL DAY
Traditional Sunday Spit Roast !!

Meetings or special occasions ?
The Board Room and The Library, will be available for private dining and meetings from the end of October.

Our menu is flexible – if we have the raw ingredients we will be happy to accommodate your desires. All our VEGETARIAN dishes are prepared without the use of animal products

Glenbervie Beef
Glenbervie Beef is from Europe's top herd – 100% Certified Aberdeen Angus, Award winning Glenbervie sets the standard for food hygiene.

PUDDINGS & CHEESE

Apple & Ginger Crumble with Double Cream	3.50
Pot of Chocolate	3.50
American Cheesecake	3.50
Selection of Cheese	4.25

A Service charge of 12.5 % will be added to all table bills. This is discretionary and is distributed to all the staff - if you are not happy with the service please remove this from your bill and let us know how we can do better. VAT is inclusive at 17.5%
The Contented Vine PLC.
17 Sussex Street London SW1V 4RR.
Tel : 0171 834 0044

THE CONTENTED VINE is open, serving food all day, Monday to Saturday 11.00 till 11.00.
Sunday we open from 11.00am till 5.00pm. We are closed on Sunday evening.
We are open for Morning Coffee or Afternoon tea - with Freshly baked Croissants and other goodies.
Herbal, Fruit and Leaf teas are available – ask to see the box !!!

October 2010

THE BRASSERIE at THE CONTENTED VINE

STARTERS

Freshly made Soup of the day with Herbed Crostini	4.50
Crispy Duck Egg with Pied De Mouton Mushrooms	6.00
Classic Prawn Cocktail	6.50
Char Grilled Calamari with Chick Peas Puree and Sweet Chilli Sauce	7.00
Chicken Liver Paté with Cumberland Sauce and Melba Toast	6.50
Quail Eggs with Celery Salt	5.00
"Croquetas Jamon"	6.50
Deep Fried Artichoke with Pine Nut Puree and Black Olive Oil	6.50
Goats Cheese Twice Baked Soufflé with Tomato Sauce	6.00

MAINS

Trio of Fishcakes, Sorrel Sauce and wilted Spinach, Green Leaf Salad OR French Fries	12.50
Roast Salmon with Dauphinoise Potatoes, Marinated Courgettes, Dill and Caper Butter Sauce	12.50
Char Grilled 10oz Scottish Sirloin Steak French Fries, Herb Leaf Salad, Parsley Butter	18.50
Scottish 8oz Chopped Steak Beef Burger, Seeded Bun Green Leaf Salad, French Fries	11.00
Penne with Spinach Cream Sauce, Sun dried Tomatoes	10.50
Served with Smoked Salmon	13.00
Breasts of Wood Pigeon with Crushed Peas and Leeks	13.50
Calves Liver served with Mash & Bacon	11.50
Slow Roasted Belly Pork, Apple Mash, Caramelised Shallots, Wilted Spinach, Honey and Oyster Jus	13.50

From the Rotisserie

Half Spit Roasted Corn Fed Chicken with Mixed Leaf Salad & French Fries OR Mash, Seasonal Vegetables & Jus	12.75

DESSERTS

Our Home Made Ice Creams: Please ask for today's' choice of flavours	6.00
Baked Chocolate Fondant Pudding with Vanilla Ice Cream	6.00
Lime and Cinnamon Crème Brulée	5.50
Chocolate Pot	5.50
Apple Crumble with Cream	5.50
Pannetone Bread & Butter Pudding with Homemade Vanilla Ice Cream	6.50

CHEESE

A Selection of five English and French Cheeses	9.00

COVER CHARGE
The cover charge of £1.25 includes freshly baked French Bread and Butter, our own Marinated Olives as well as unlimited still or sparkling water from our in house filtration system - so no nasty carbon footprint!!

12 ½ % discretionary service will be added to all table bills

---

TUESDAY TO SATURDAY FIXED PRICE LUNCH MENU
Great value with a selection of three starters, three mains and a pudding or cheese
2 X courses £12.85 Additional course £3.15

SIDE ORDERS

Crushed Peas	3.00
Mixed Vegetables	3.00
French Fries	2.75
Buttered Mash	3.00
Mixed Green Leaf/Herb leaf	3.00
Tomato and Red Onion Salad	3.00

"LE WEEKEND" AT THE CONTENTED VINE

Fixed price lunch served from 12.00 Saturday & Sunday

Twice Baked Goats Cheese Soufflé with Tomato Sauce
Homemade Soup of the Day
Scrambled Eggs with Smoked Salmon on Toast
***
Char grilled 8 oz Burger with Salad and French Fries
Grilled Breast of Chicken Escalope with CV Salad
Penne with Spinach, Sundried Tomatoes and Parmesan Shavings
***
Chocolate Pot
Mango Ice Cream with White Chocolate Shavings and Tuille Biscuit
Apple Crumble with Cream

2 Courses £12.85 OR 3 Courses £16.00

"LE WEEKEND" KIDS MENU £6.50
¼ POUND BURGER & FRIES OR FISH GOUJONS & FRIES

One scoop of homemade vanilla ice cream in a cornet or bowl

PRIVATE ROOMS

The Gallery
On the first floor is a beautiful room with high ceilings which can seat up to 24 at one large table. can seat up to 40 or hold 50 for drinks and canapés. Lunch or dinner, corporate or private, parties, receptions, birthdays or any special occasion,

The Garden & Red Room
A perfect setting for informal candlelit dinners, lunches or BBQ – smokers can sit under cover in the garden! 60+ for a canapés drinks reception, buffet or party.

Whatever your event, please ask for a copy of The Contented Vine Private Dining Menus – or download from our website:
www.contentedvine.com

THE CONTENTED VINE

14. "CONTENTED CHUMS!!!"

MEL & GARY DONS 60th!!

YVONNE CHAMPAGNE BOLINGER

THE CONTENTED VINE

ANNA

BRUCE TYRRELL & PATRICK NALLY

SUE AND MARGARET

ANDREW AND ANNA

CHEF DAMIAN

CERI

SPECIAL THANKS

CHEFS DAMIAN & KAROL PLUS KITCHEN GENERAL WONDER SAMPATH
ANNA – FOR 6 OR 7 YEARS HEPING KEEP KATE SANE ('ISH)
LOUISA (COKTAIL MENACE – THANX FOR THE HEADACHES)
NETTIE DEAN (SUMS / PINO GRIGIO CLUB)
MICK DEAN (ARISTE EXTRAORDINAIRE)
JANE (KATES MUM) AND SISTER CLARE (FOR FAMILY RECIPES)
SUE HALL (FOR GREAT HELP WITH THE EDITING)
MARGARET (FAVOURITE CUSTOMER AWARD!) FOR JUST BEING MARGARET

WE WERE LUCKY ENOUGH TO HAVE SOME REALLY SPECIAL WINE SUPPLIERS WHO BECAME (IF THEY WERE NOT ALREADY) GREAT FRIENDS:

JUSTIN LLEWELLYN at CHAMPAGNE TAITTINGER
JAMES PRICE at GENESIS WINES
CLIVE ASHBY at HALLGARTEN WINES
CHARLES RIDLER at CHAMPAGNE LAURENT PERRIER
BROUGH GUERNY RANDALL at E W LOEB

PLUS
PAM MORRIS-SYKES FOR BEING THERE WHEN WE NEEDED HER!
SOLICITOR EXTRAORDINAIRE AND GOOD FRIEND JULIAN GOULDING
WEB SITE WONDER AND TECH KING NEIL BATCHELOR
DEBBIE ARMET FROM BARCLAYS CORPORATE

IN CHAMPAGNE
NICOLE SNOZZI AT LAURENT PERRIER, OLIVIER DE LA GIRAUDIERE AT LANSON, HUBERT DE BILLY AND HIS FATHER CHRISTIAN AT POL ROGER, FREDRICK HEIDSIECK AT LOUIS ROEDERER, YVES DELAITTRE AT MUMM & CHRISTIAN HOLTHAUSEN AT PIPER HEIDSIECK

IN AUSTRALIA:
OZ CLARKE, DOUG LEEHMAN, GORDON GEBBIE, GEOFF MERRIL, BRUCE TYRRELL & THE INDOMITABLE HAZEL MURPHY

THANKS GUYS ... IT WAS FUN!!

THE CONTENTED VINE

CHAMPAGNE ACADEMY DINNER 2010

E-mail: info@contentedvine.com
www.contentedvine.com

INDEX

STARTERS

CALAMARI	8
CHICKEN LIVER PATE	8
CRAB CAKES	8
CROQUETAS JAMON	9
FRENCH ONION SOUP	9
TWICE BAKED GOATS CHEESE SOUFFLÉ	10
PARMESAN CUSTARD	11
PARMESAN BRULÉE	11

LIGHT BITES

ARTICHOKE AND GOATS CHEESE TART	12
PEA SPINACH AND RICOTTA FILO TART	12
CHICKEN WINGS	13
GNOCHI	13
POTATO PURÉE	13
PIGEON BREAST A LA PETIT POIS	14
PORK PIE	14

MAINS

BURGERS	16
MINI BURGERS	16
COQ AU VIN	16
FISHCAKES	17
SPINACH FISHCAKE SAUCE	18
FRESH PASTA	18
IBIZAN LAMB	19
INDIVIDUAL PARMEGIANI MELANZONE	19
LAMB TAGINE	20
MUSHROOM TAGINE	20
NORMANDY PORK	21
PORK BELLY	21
RAGU	22
STEAK PIE	23
THE FAMILY CHICKEN PIE	23
BÉCHAMEL SAUCE	24
CHICKEN GRAVY	24

PUDDINGS

AMERICAN CHEESECAKE	25
BAKED CHOCOLATE PUDDING	25
BREAD AND BUTTER PUDDING	25
CHERRY AND ALMOND TART	26
CHOCOLATE POT	27
CHOCOLATE SAUCE FOR ICE CREAM	27
CHOCOLATE TART	27
LEMON TART	28
MARQUISE CHOCOLATE CAKE	28
CARAMEL BRITTLE	29
PAVLOVA	29
ITALIAN DACQUIRE	29
PROFITEROLES	30
STEAM PUDDING	31
TARTE TATIN	32
ICE CREAM	33
HONEYCOMB ICE CREAM	34
CHRISTMAS PUDDING ICE CREAM	34
CHOCOLATE FORT	34
CRÈME BRULÉE	35
DANISH APPLE CAKE	35
APPLE SLICE	35

CANANPÉS & NIBBLES

BOUCHÉES	56
BRUSCHETTA	56
PRAWN COCKTAIL	57
CHEESE CROUTON – FOR SOUPS AND SALADS	57
FISH GOUJONS	57
MINI SCOTCH EGGS	58
PARMESAN CRISPS	58
PARMESAN BISCUITS	58
ROAST MUSHROOM AND SAGE TARTS	59

THE CONTENTED VINE

VEGETARIAN

DAUPHINOISE POTATOES	60
FIG TARTE TATIN	60
PUMPKIN, BEAN AND COUS COUS SALAD	60
HOMEMADE CHIPS	61
POMMES PONT NEUF	61
CHICKPEA PURÉE	61
RED CABBAGE CASSEROLE	62
RICE N PEAS	62
SPANISH POTATOES	63
STUFFING	63
POTATO PURÉE	64
ACKEE	64
INDIAN SPICED RICE SALAD.	65
PERRIN'S CORN PUDDING	66

CAKES, BISCUITS, BREADS & PIZZAS

CHOCOLATE CHIP COOKIES	67
COFFEE AND WALNUT CAKE	67
FRUIT SCONES	67
CHOCOLATE CAKE	68
CHOCOLATE GANACHE	68
KENTUCKY GINGERBREAD	68
FUDGE ICING	69
VICTORIA SPONGE CAKE	69
PIZZA	70
BASIC PIZZA DOUGH	70
FOCACCIA	71
5 MINUTE FOCCACIA	71

DRESSINGS, SAUCES, STOCKS & JAM

BREAD SAUCE	72
BURGER RELISH	72
COCONUT DRESSING	72
CRANBERRY & ROAST SHALLOT CHUTNEY	72
CRANBERRY, PORT AND ORANGE RELISH	73
HOLLANDAISE SAUCE	73
PRESERVED LEMONS	74
QUICK CHICKEN STOCK	74
LAMB OR BEEF STOCK	74
SWEET CORN RELISH	75
TARTAR SAUCE	75
VEGETABLE STOCK	75
JERK MARINADE	76
MY JERK RECIPE	76
STRAWBERRY JAM	76
RINDLESS LEMON MARMALADE	77
APRICOT JAM	77